Mandalas Coloring Book

✓ **50** Adorable **coloring pages** ▪

✓ **Great for** young **artists and** adults ♟

✓ **Ideal for** crayons, markers, **or colored** pencils ✏

✓ Large print **page format:** 8.5 x 11 inches ▪

✓ Single-sided **pages to avoid bleed-through, ensuring your masterpieces remain pristine** ◗

✓ **Calming and relaxing activity to explore creativity** ♥

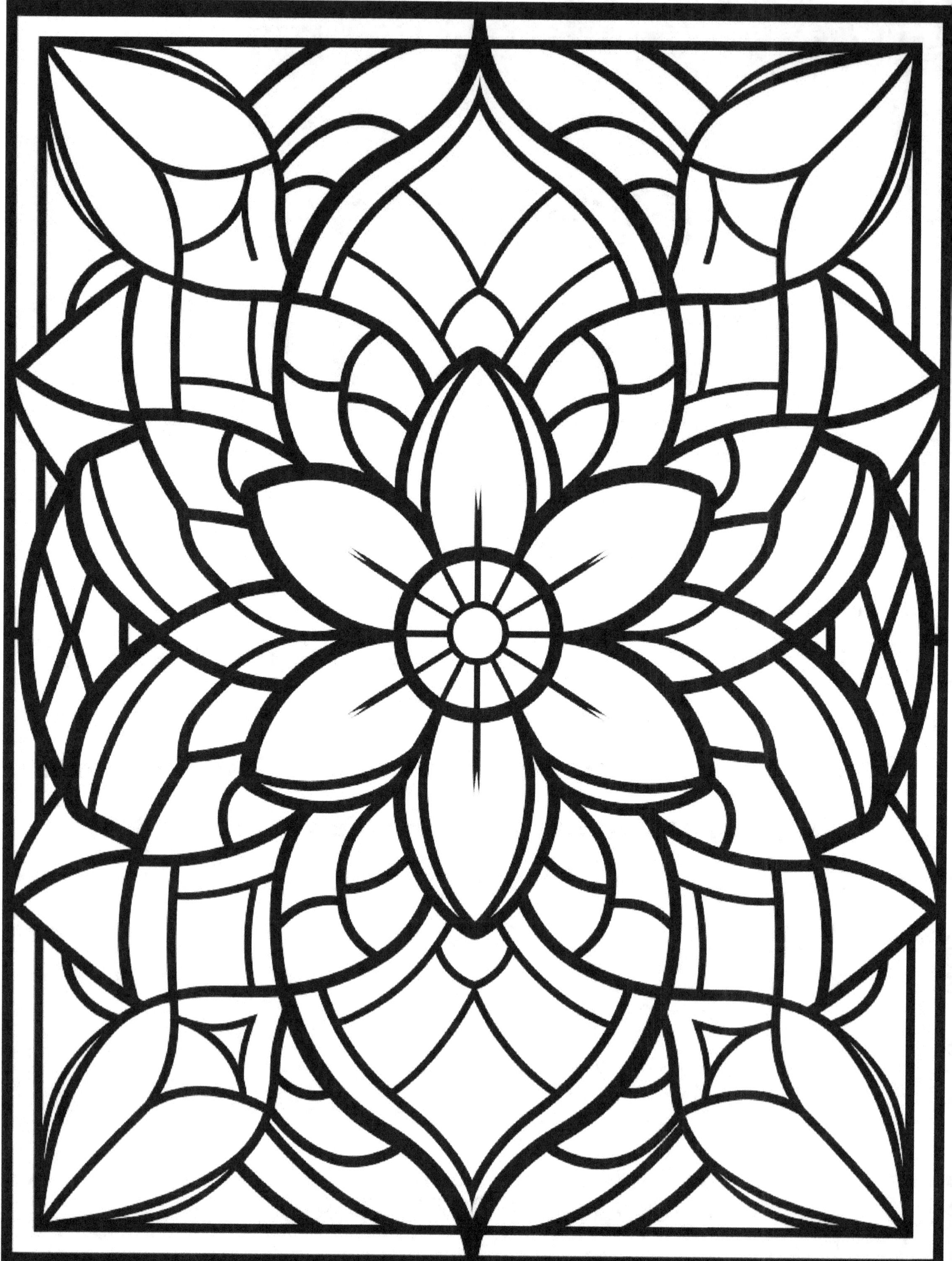

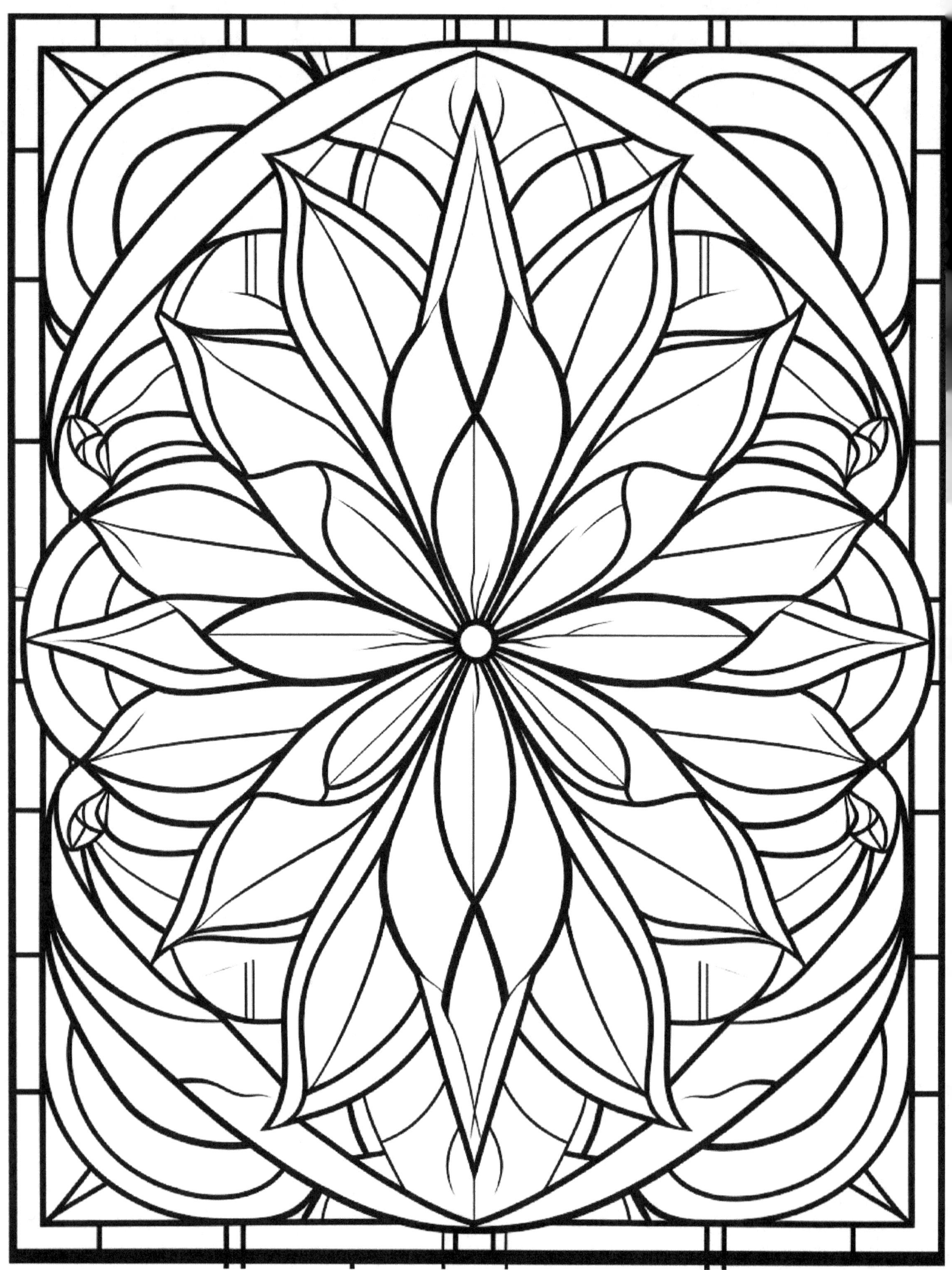

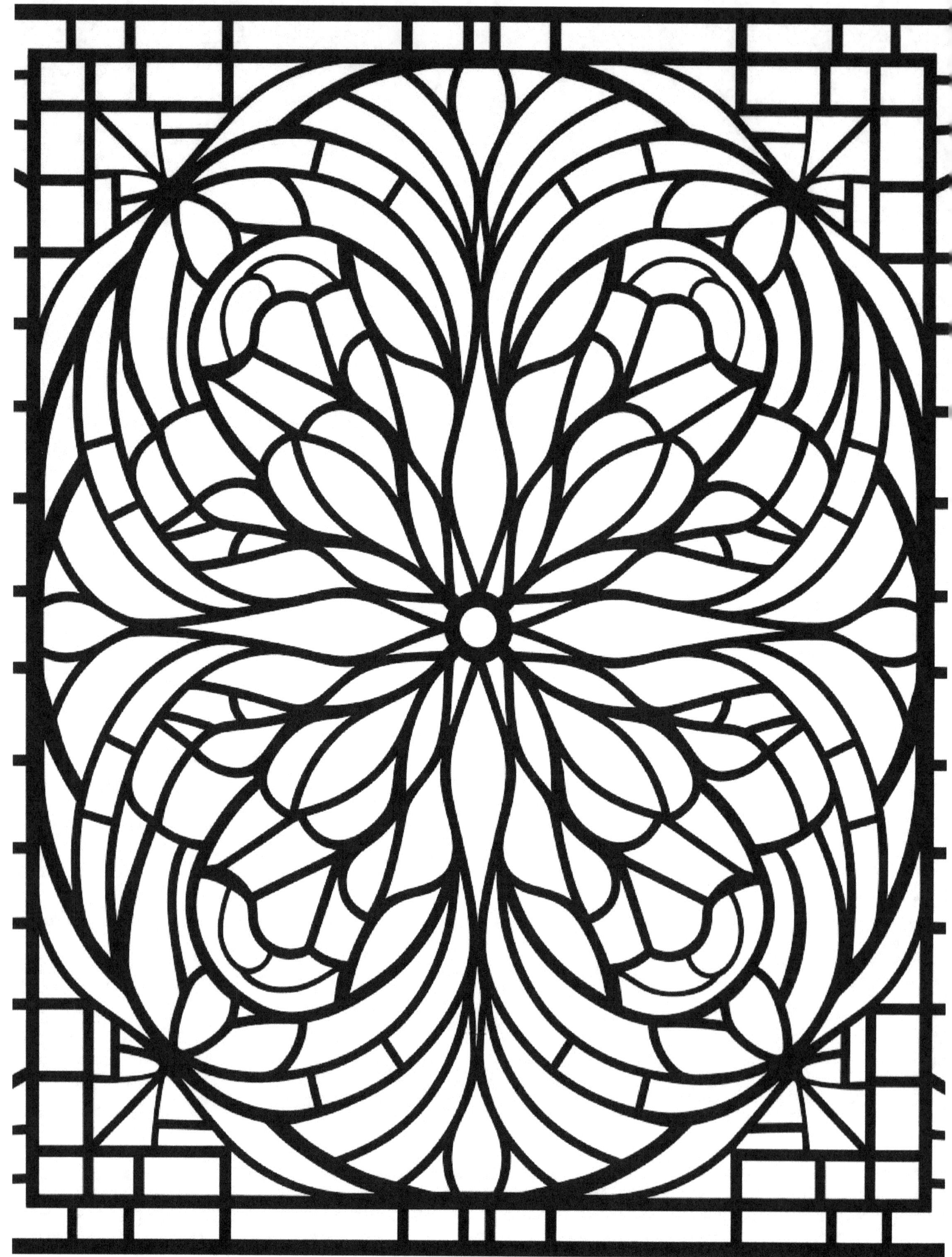

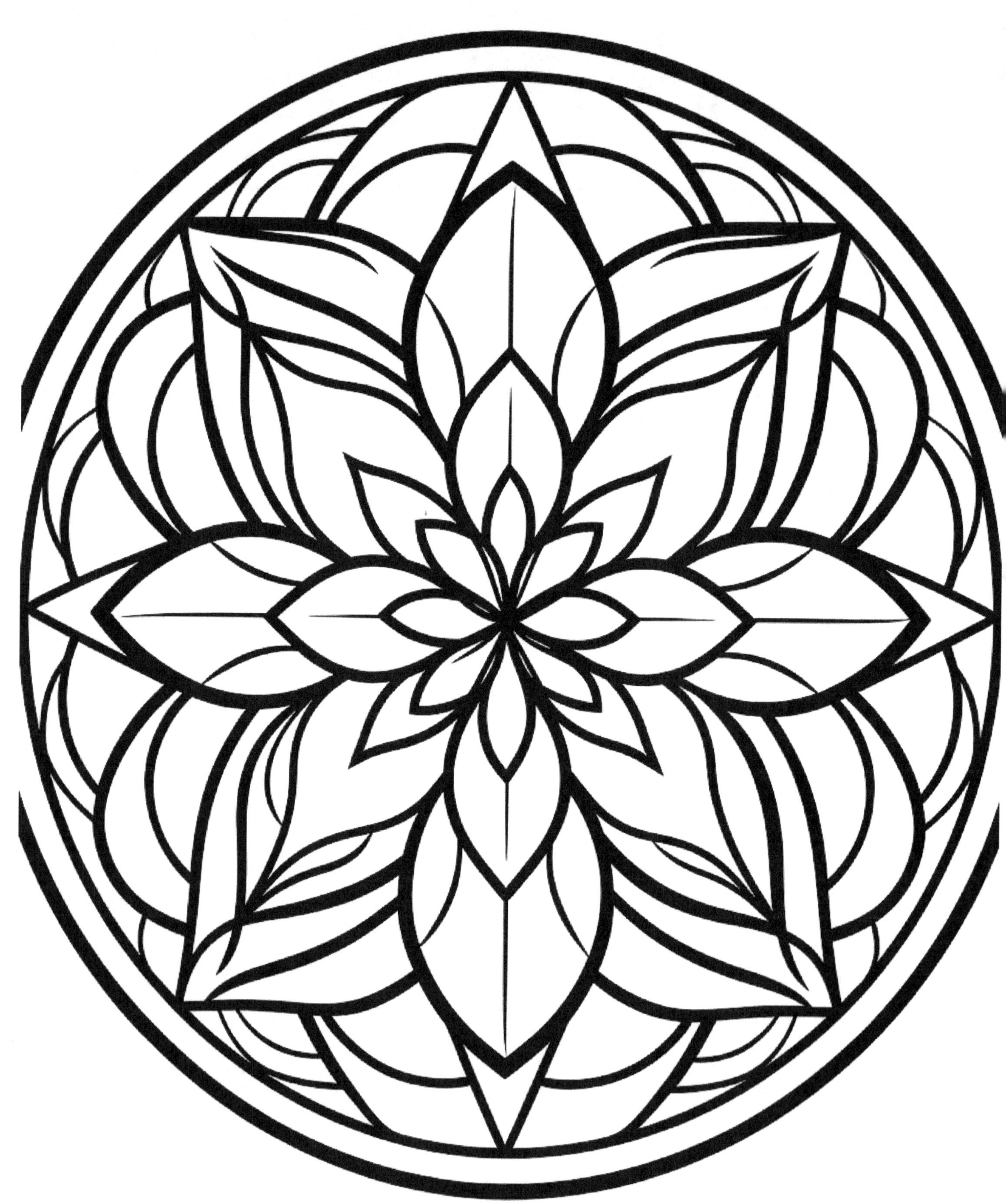

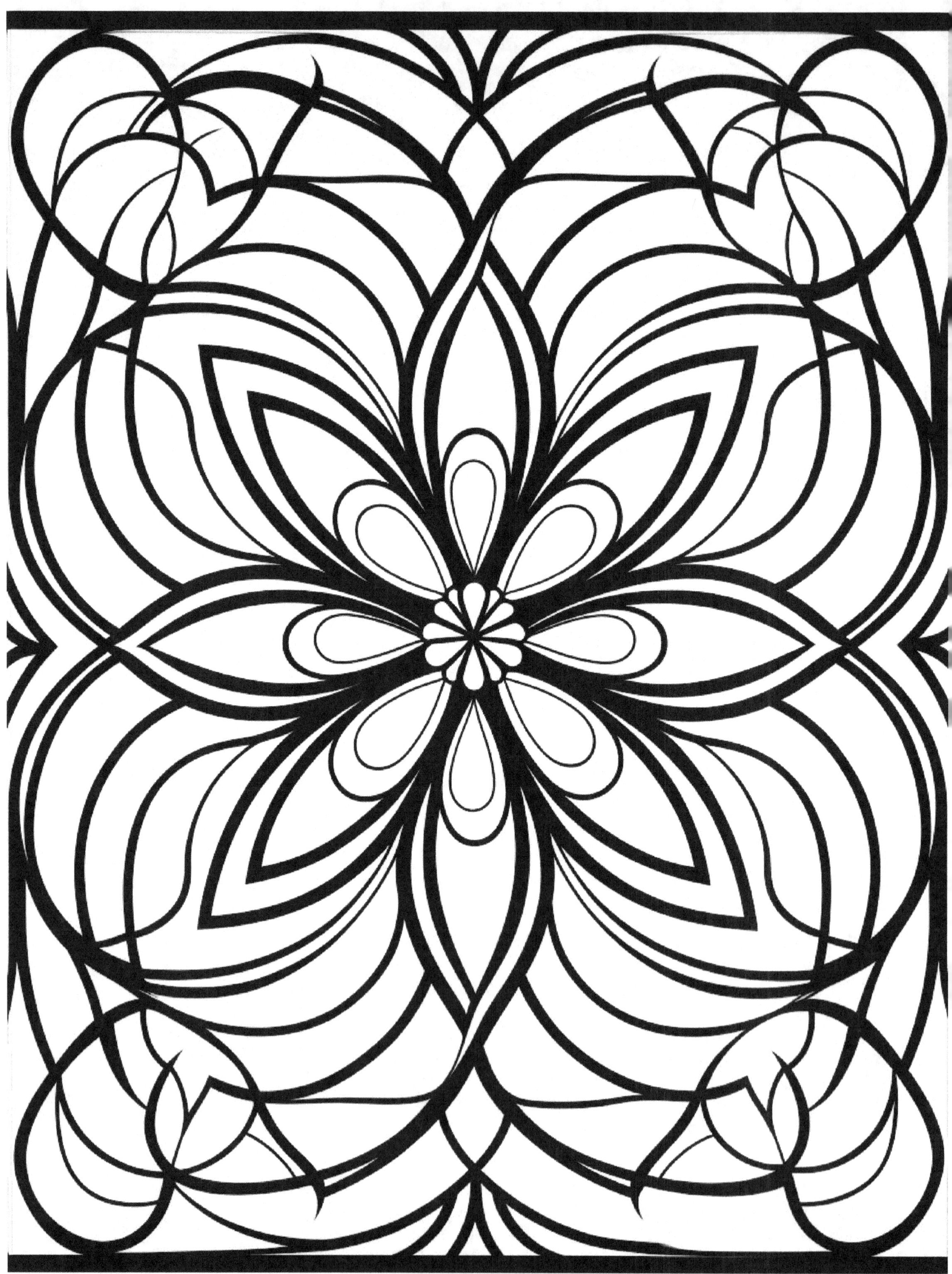

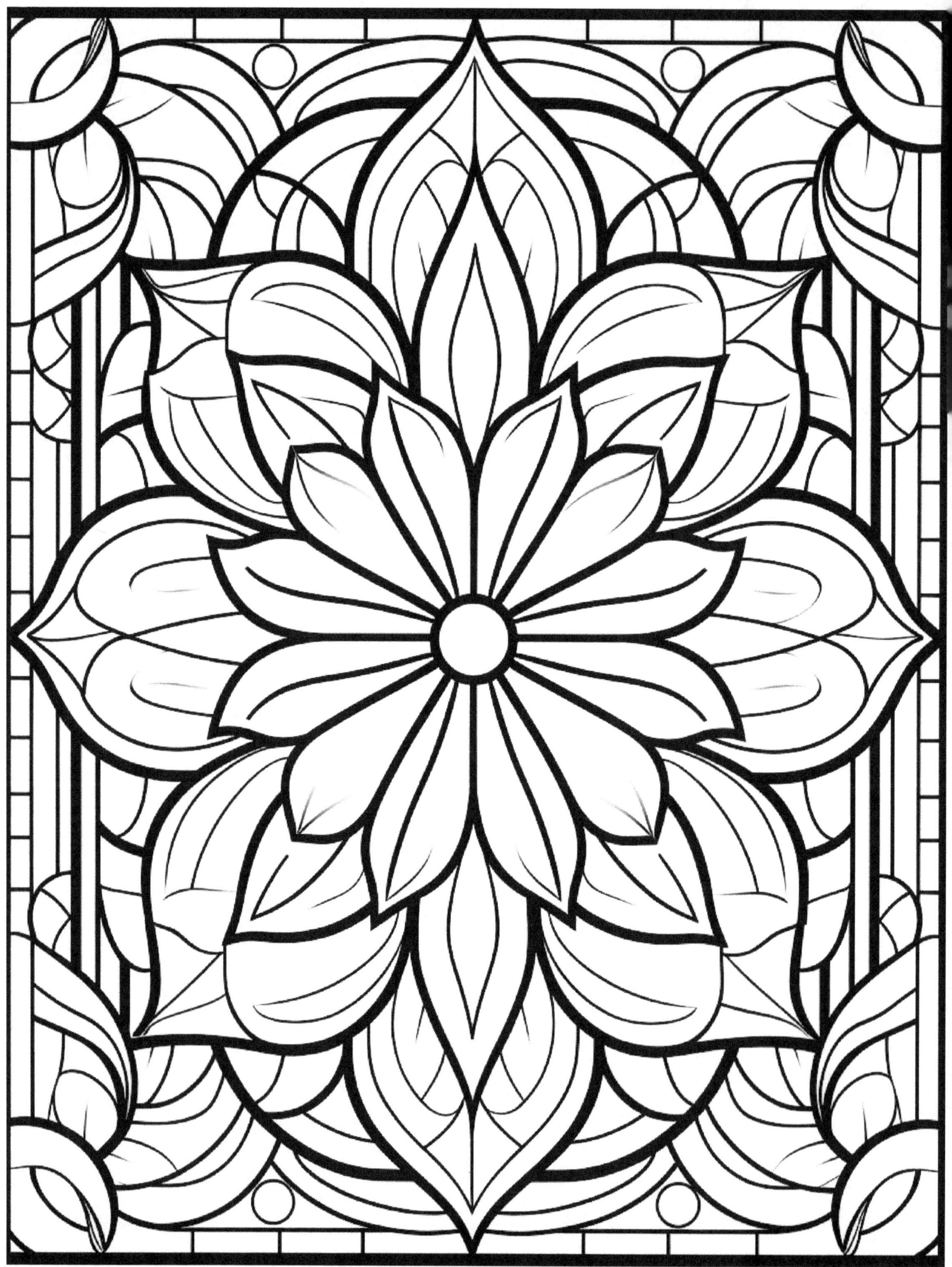

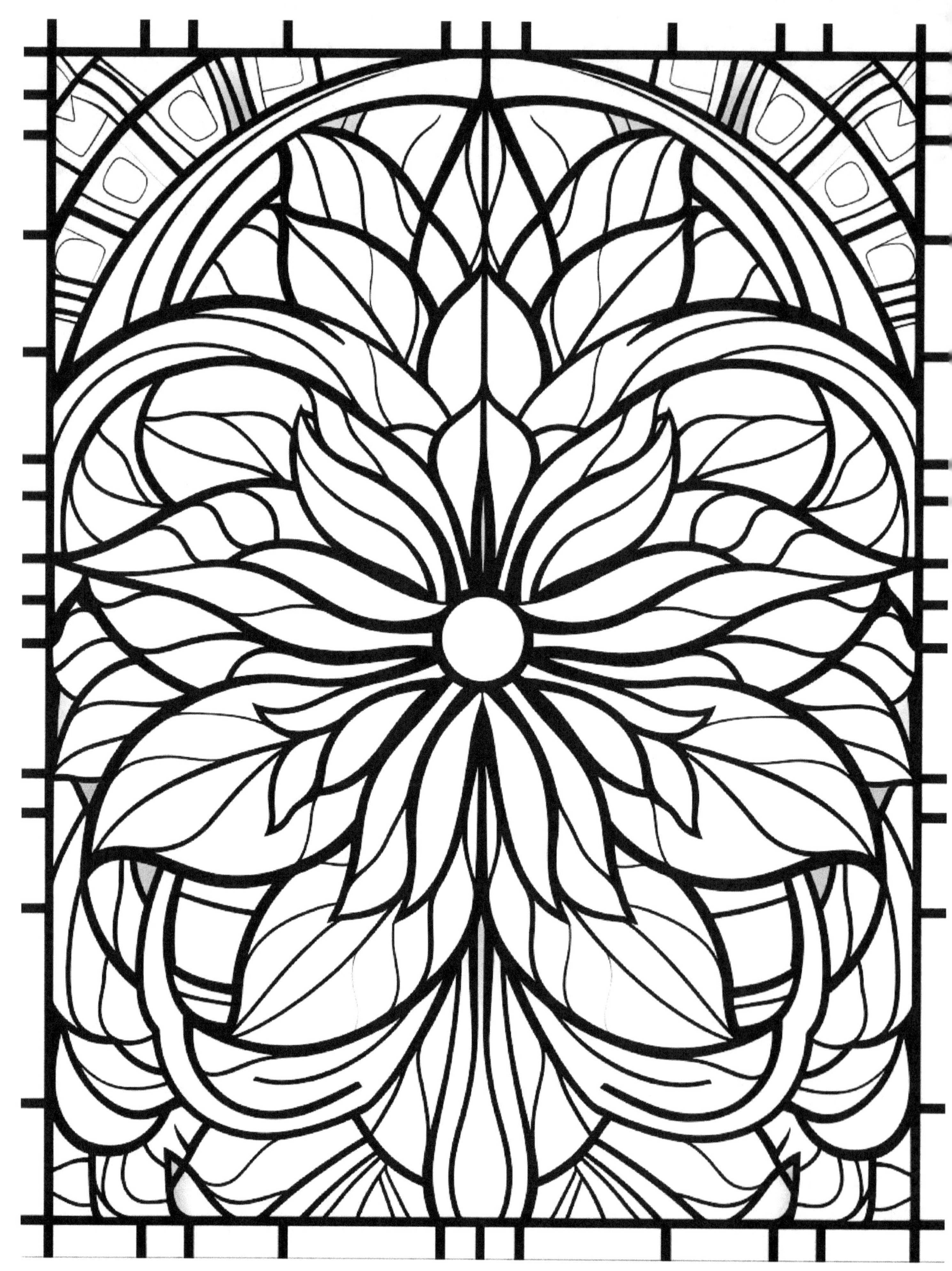

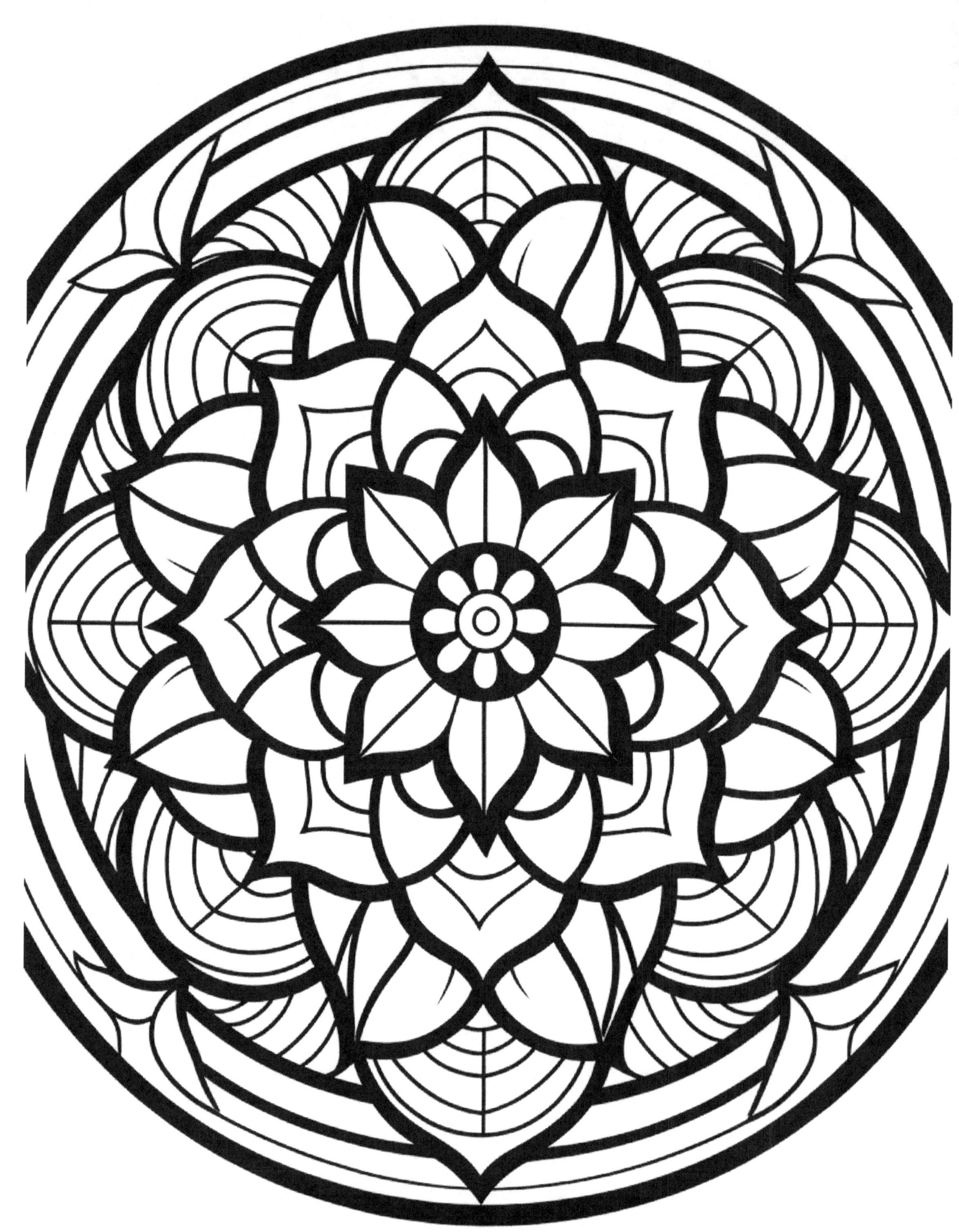

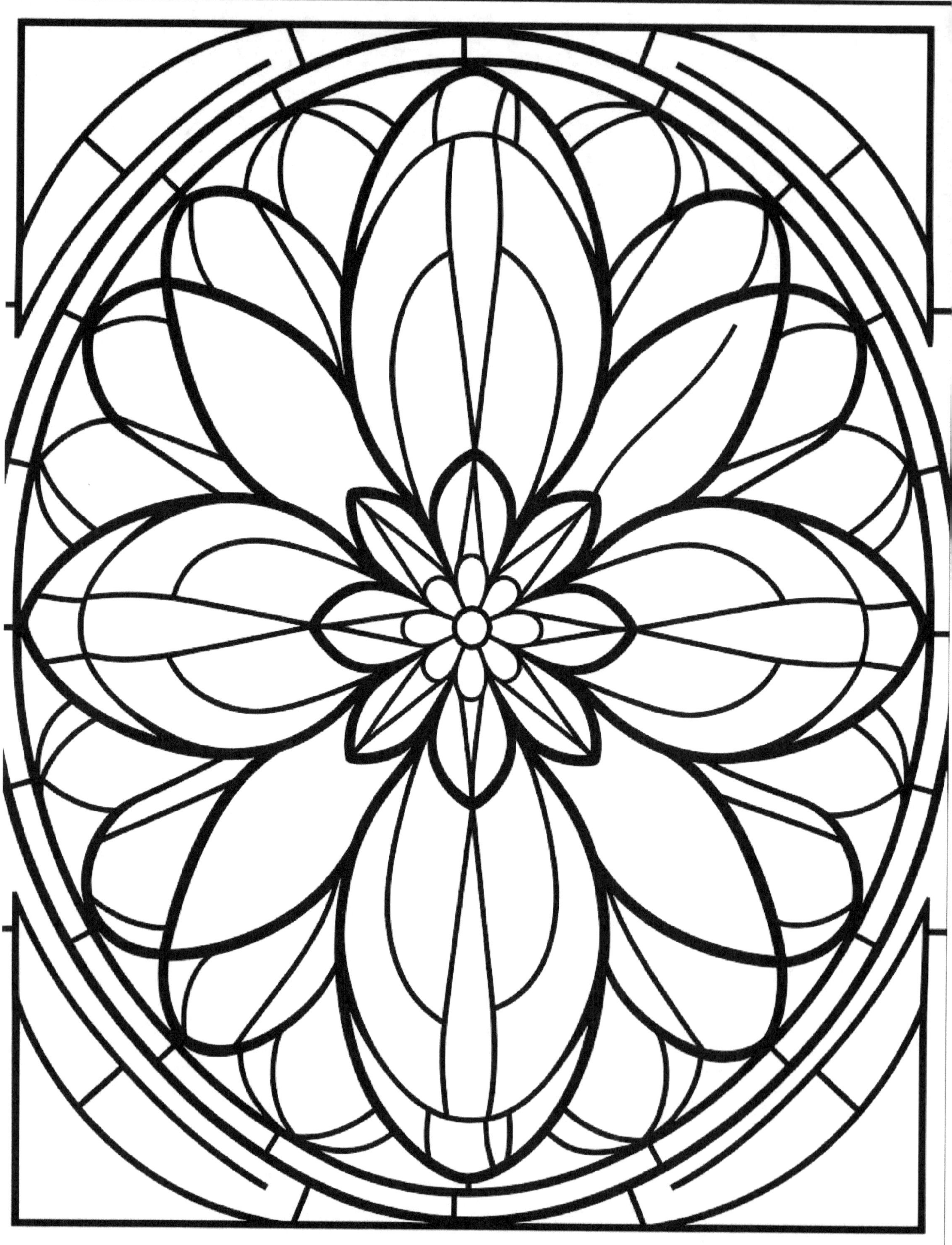

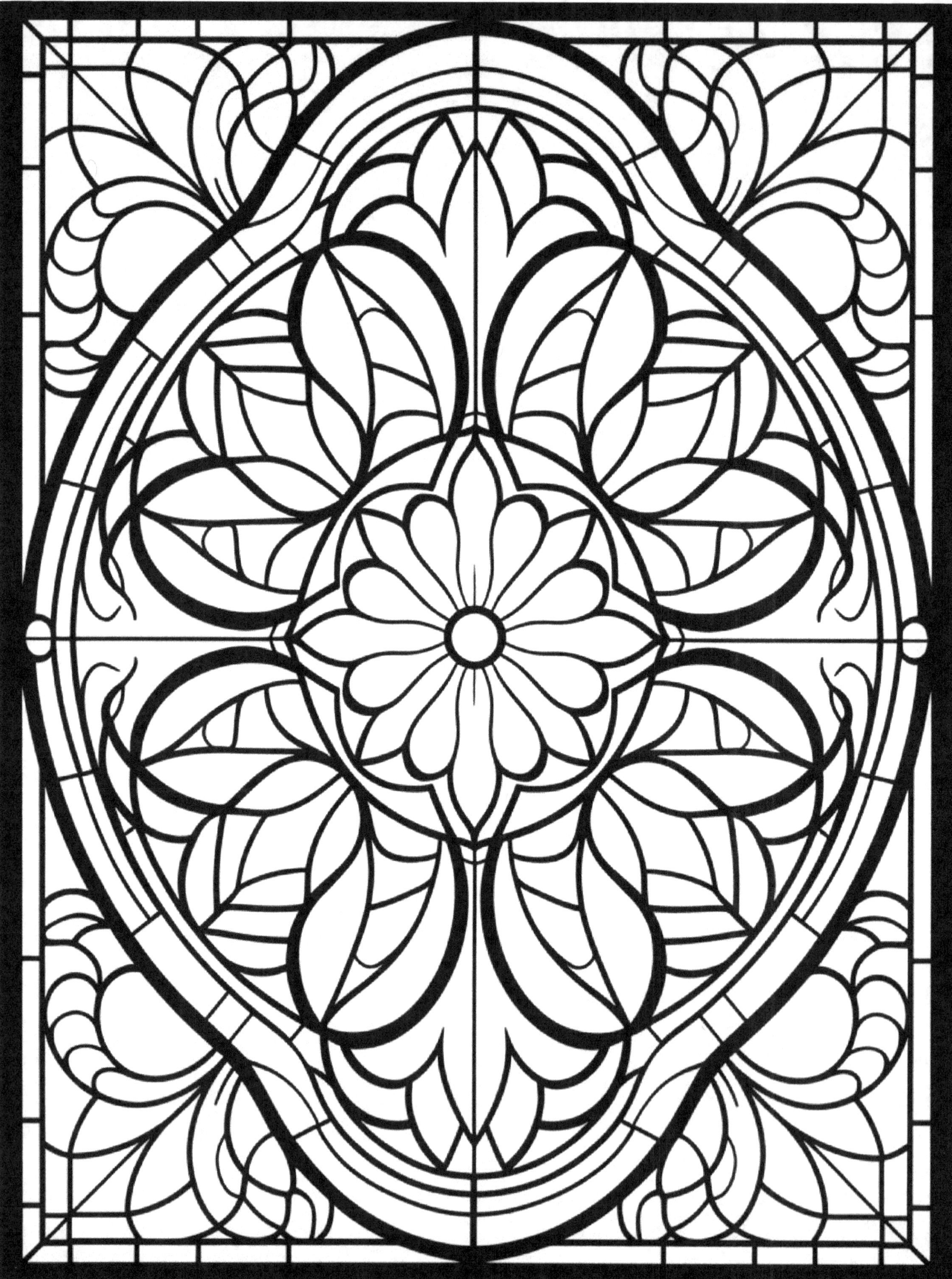

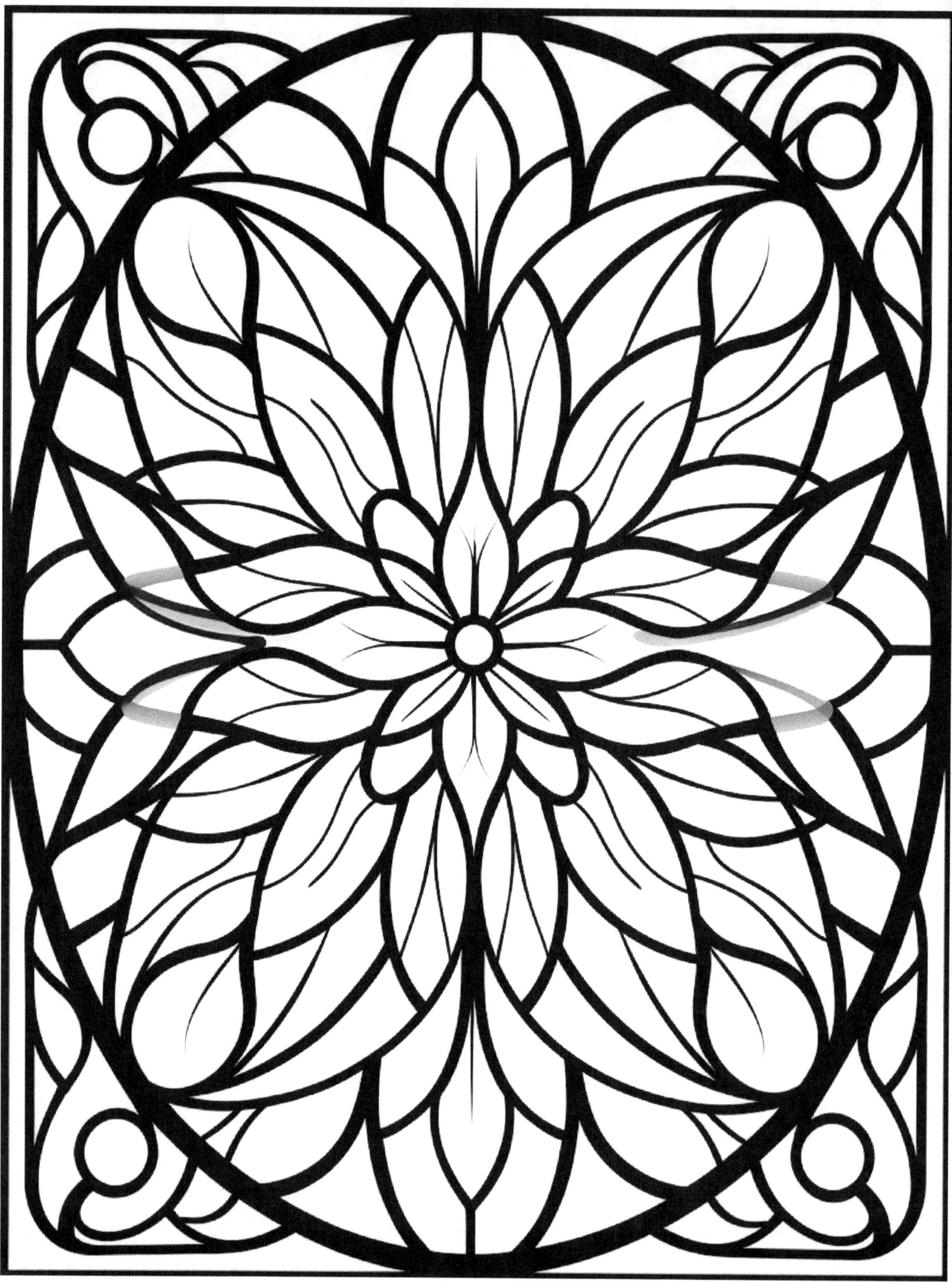

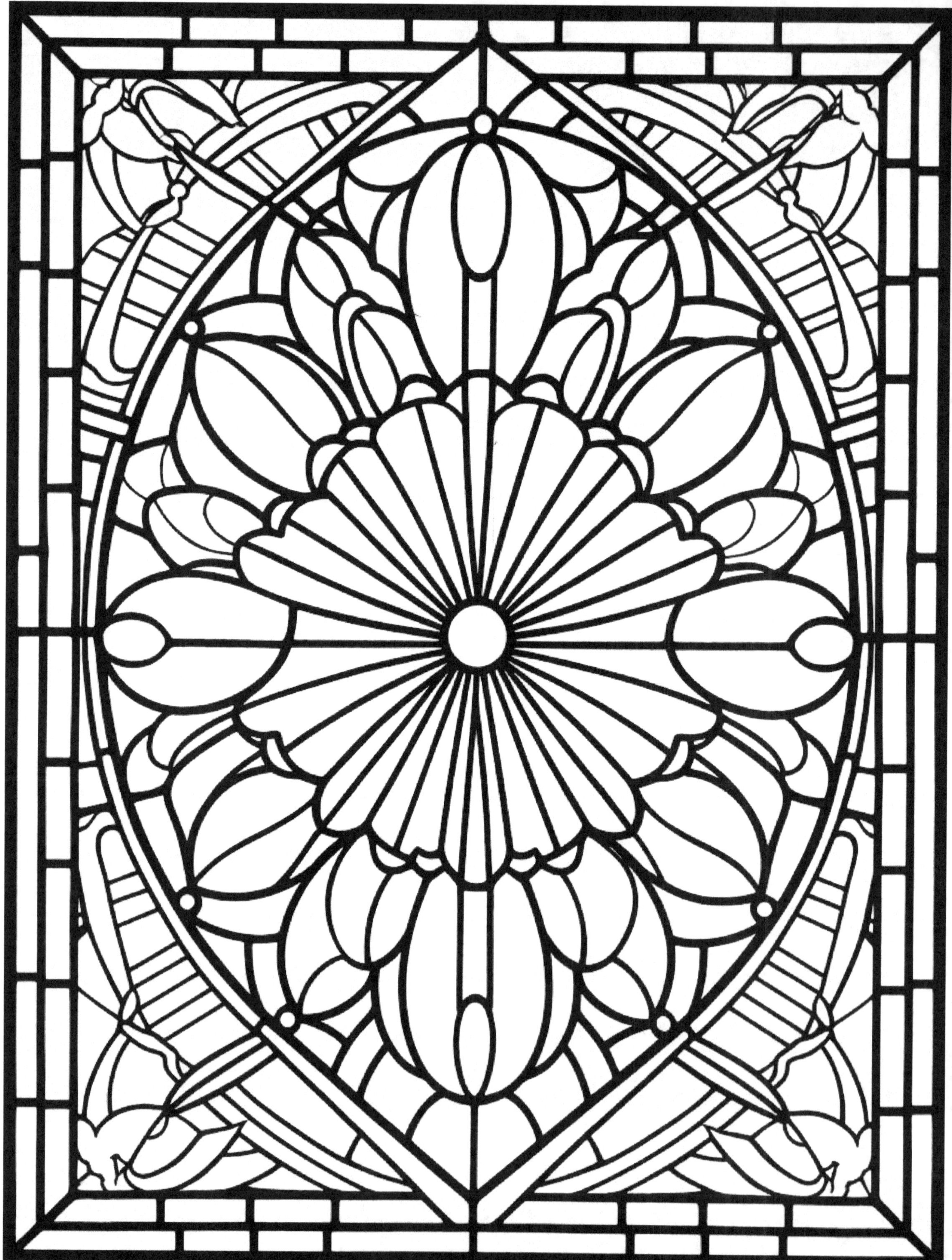

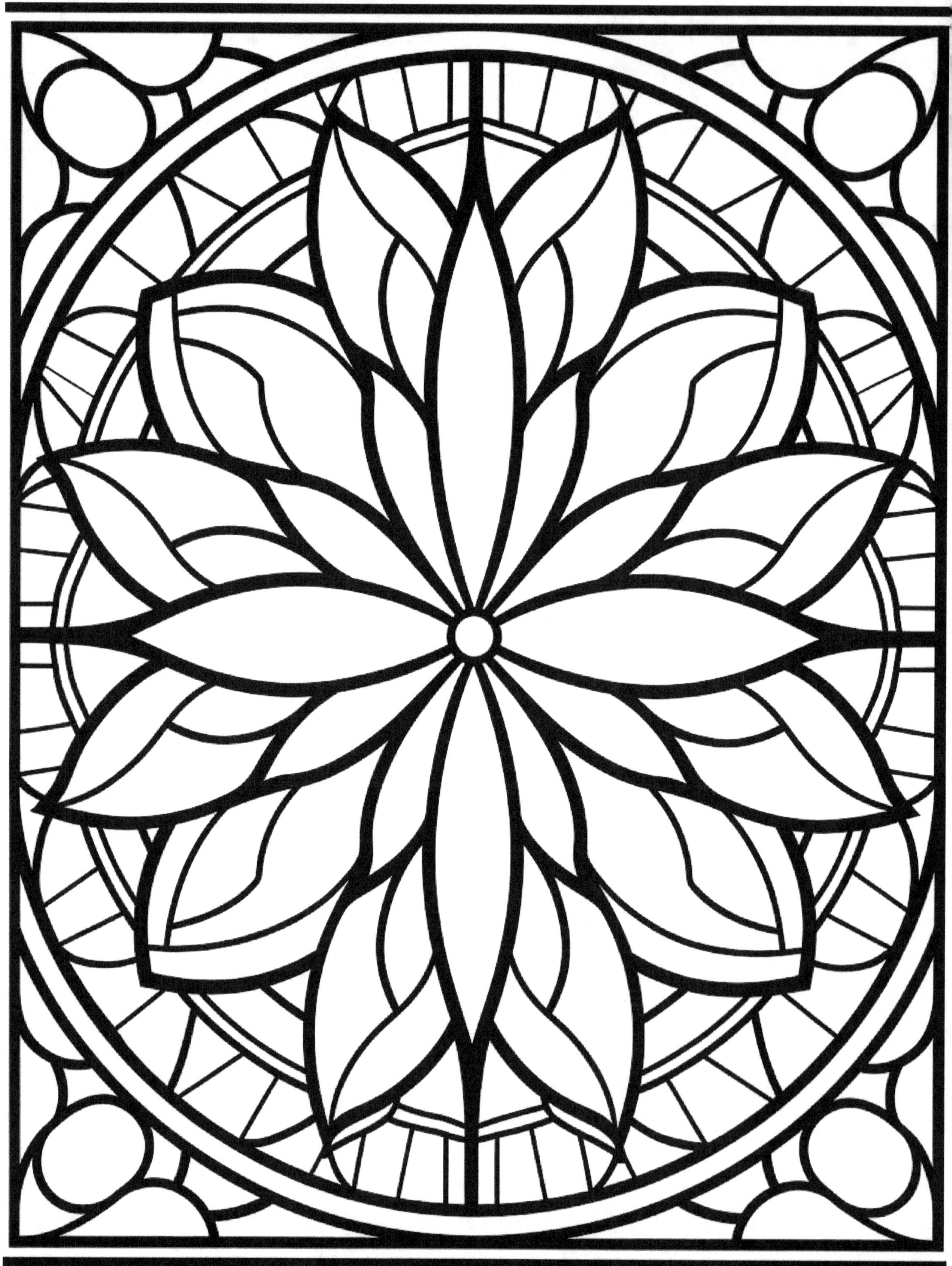

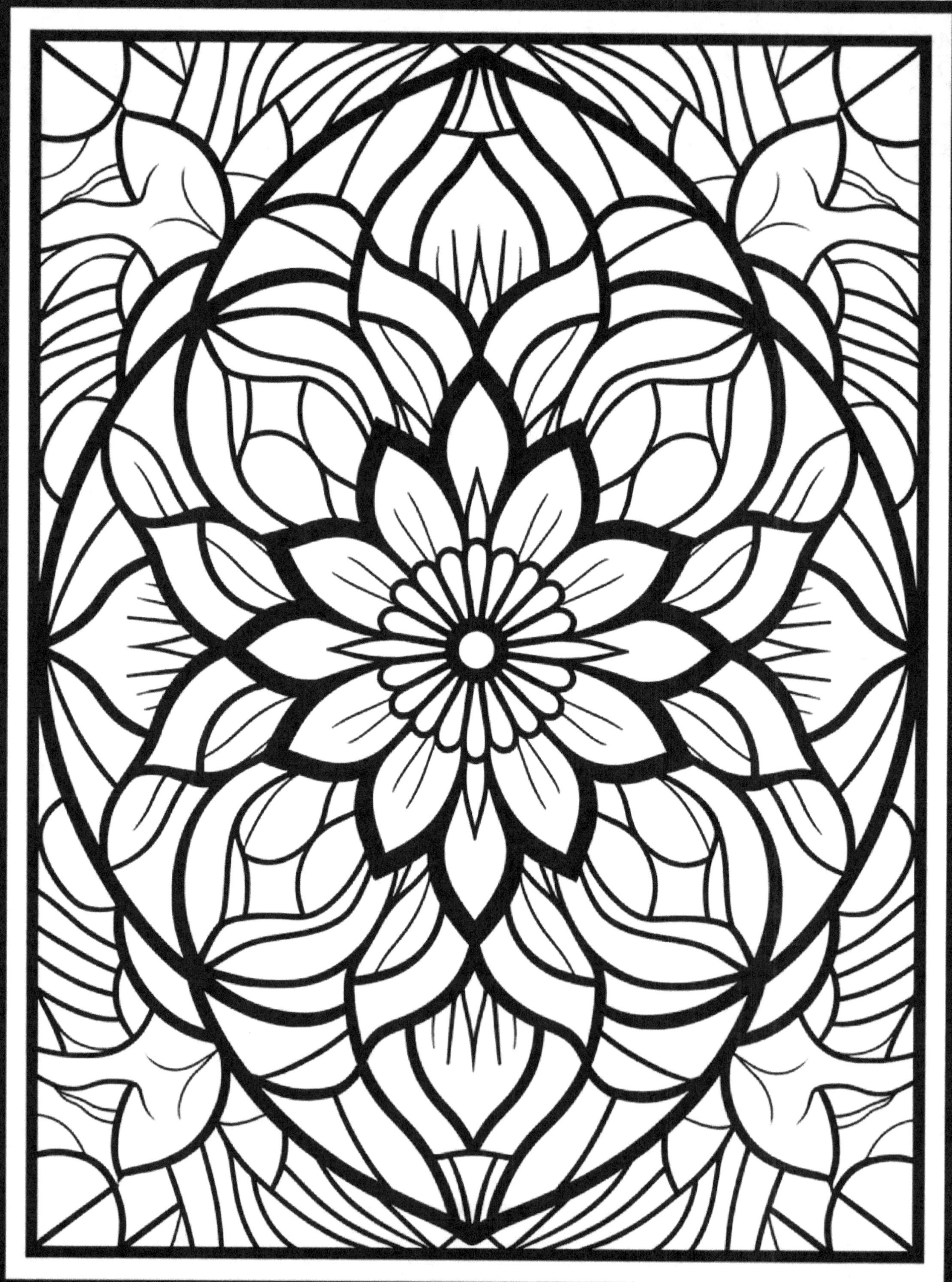

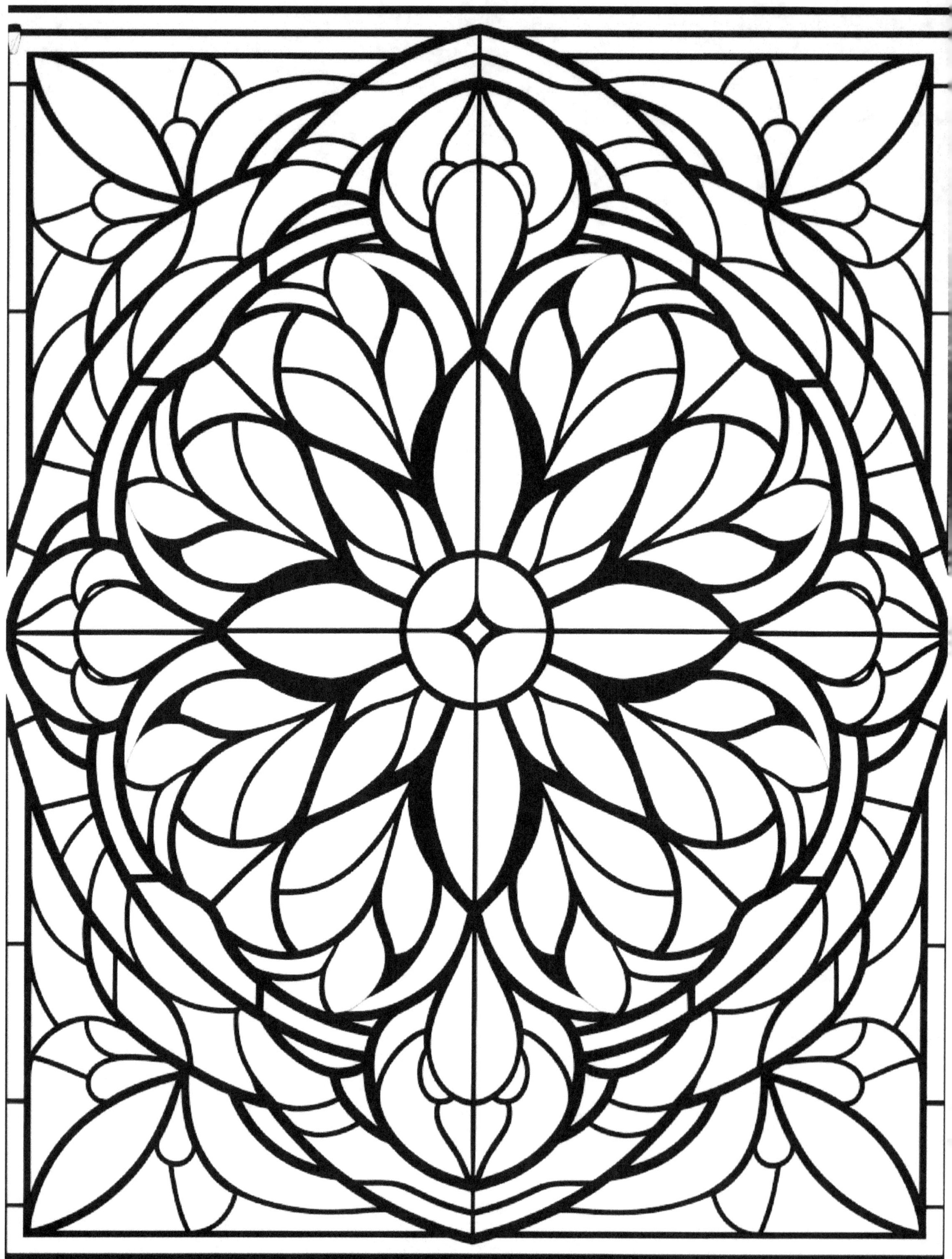

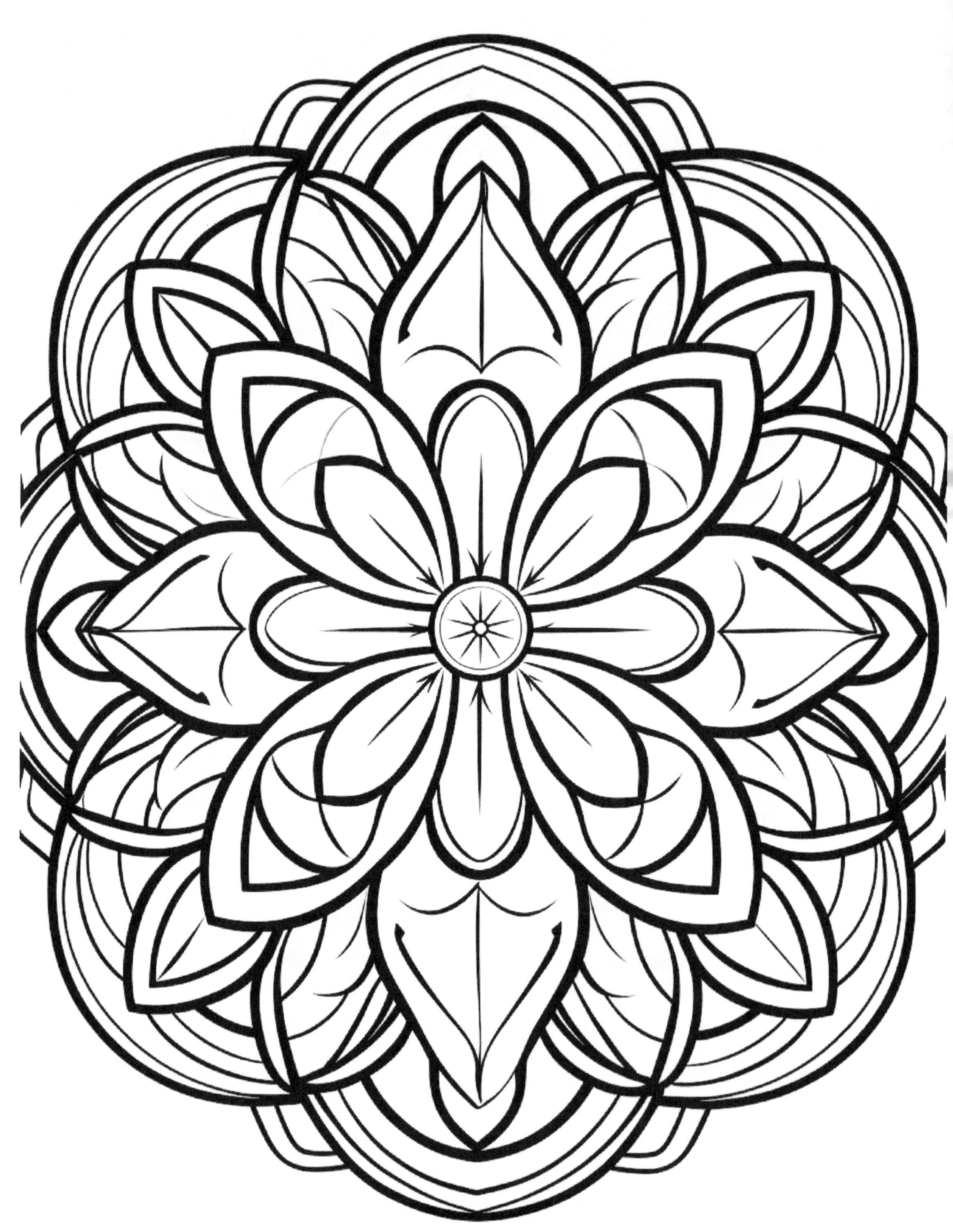

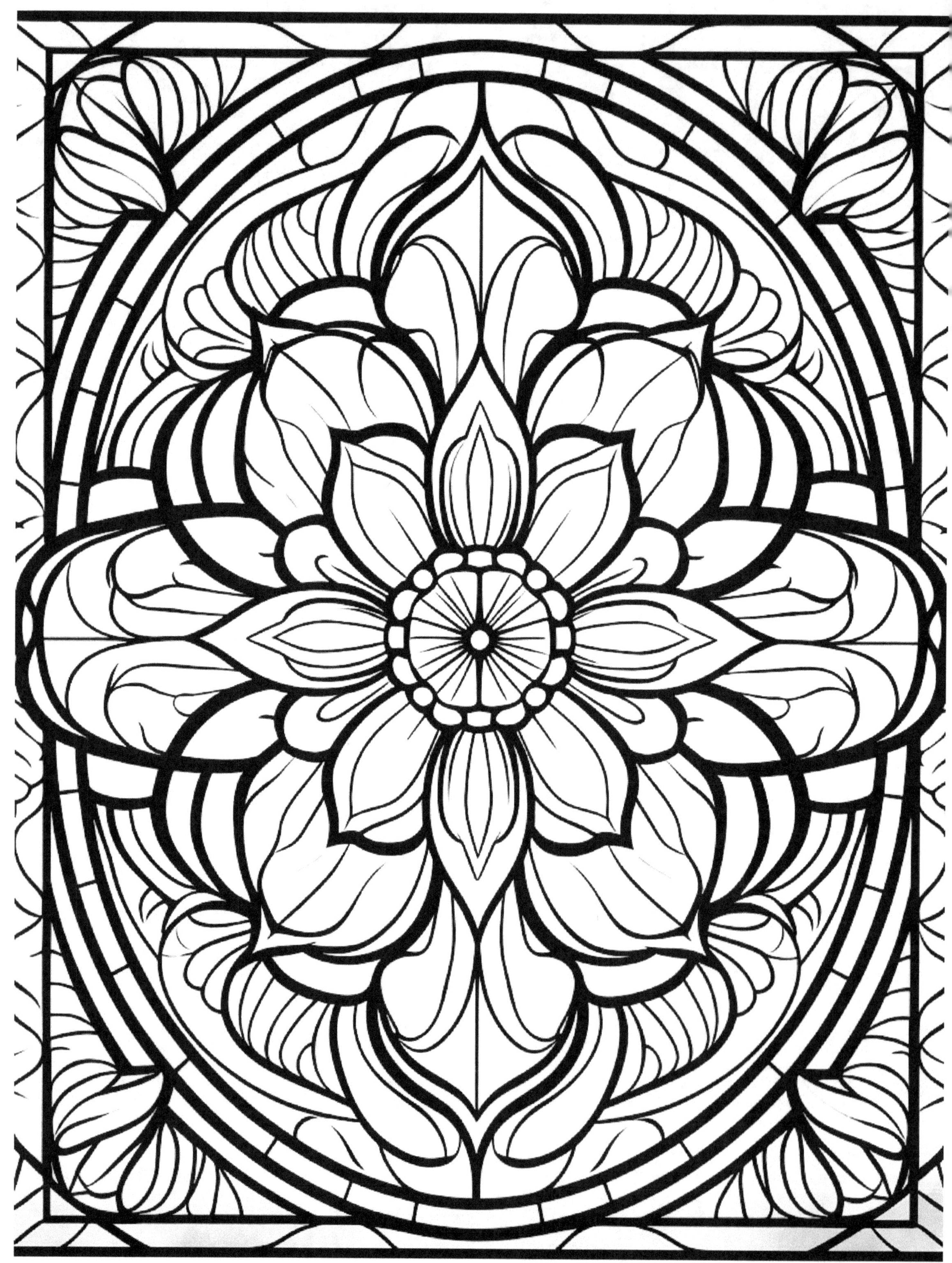

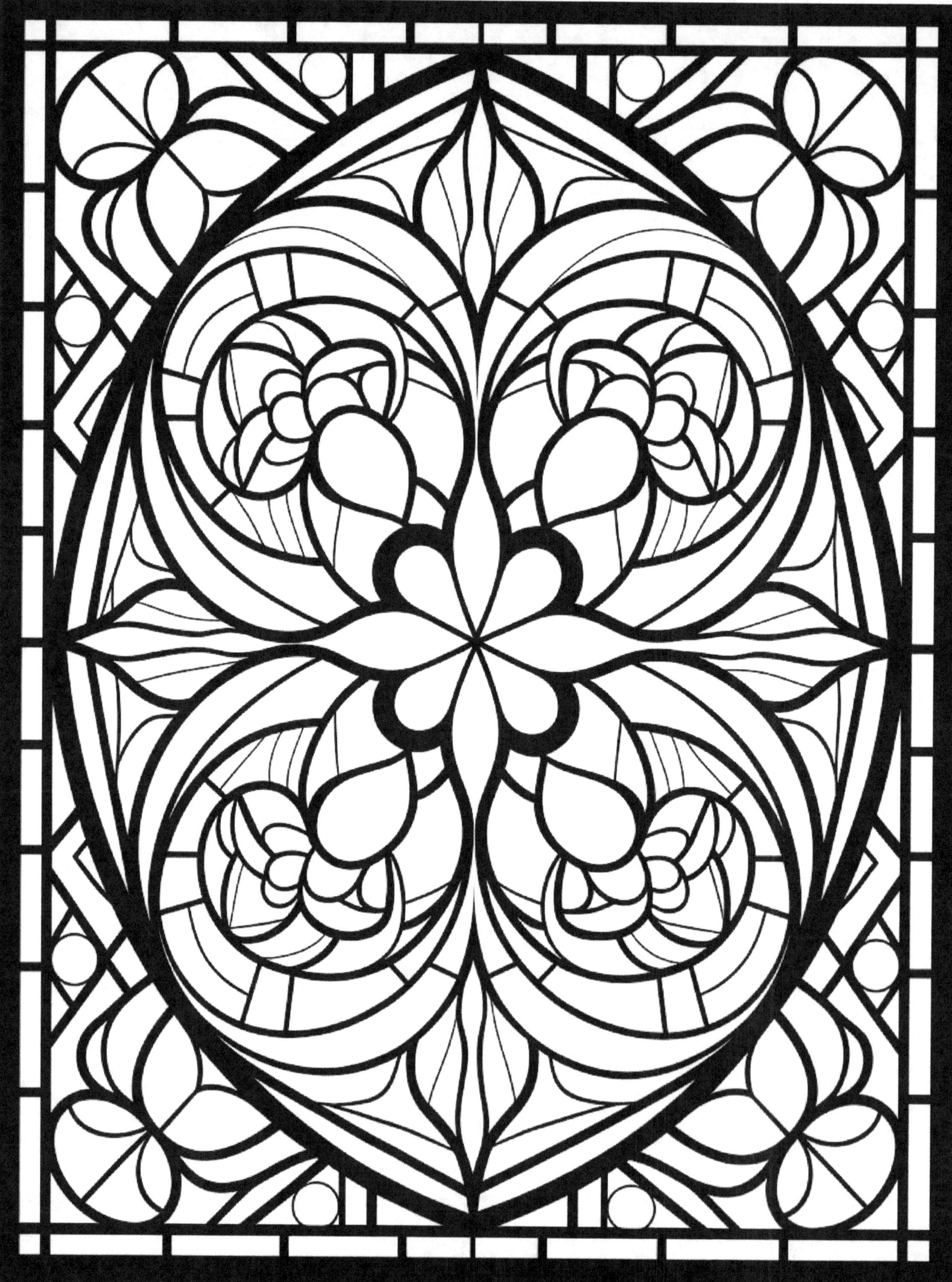

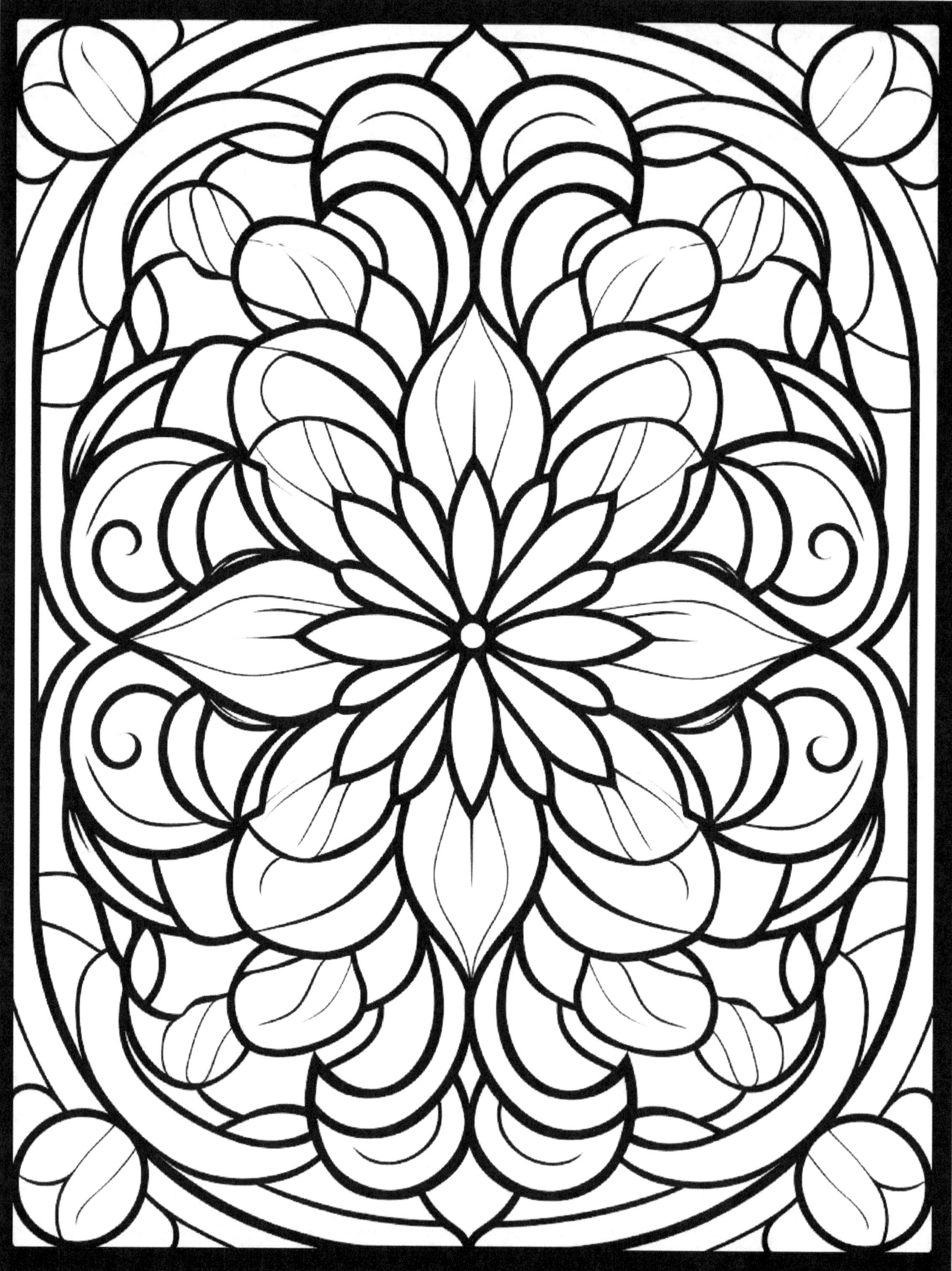

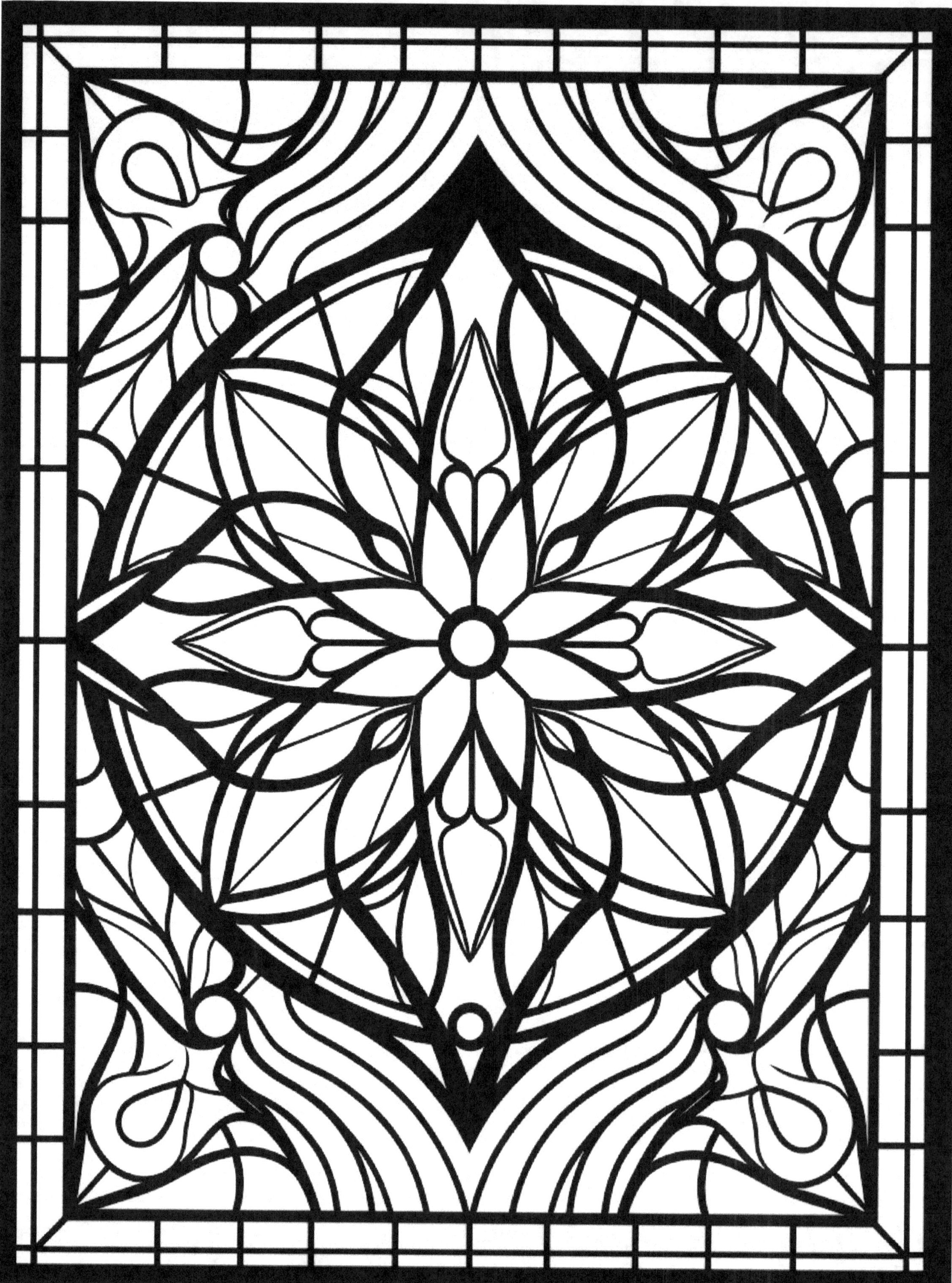

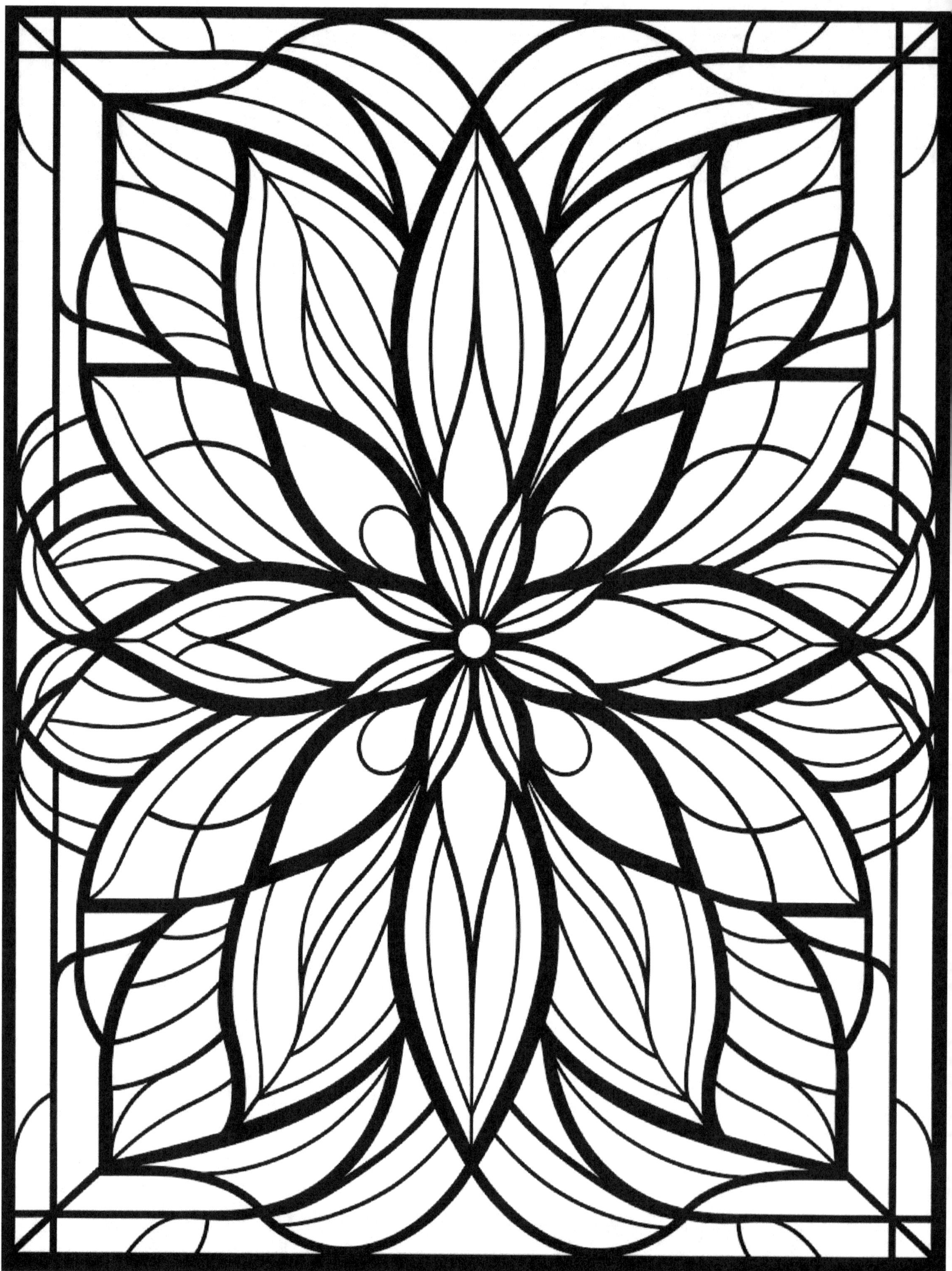

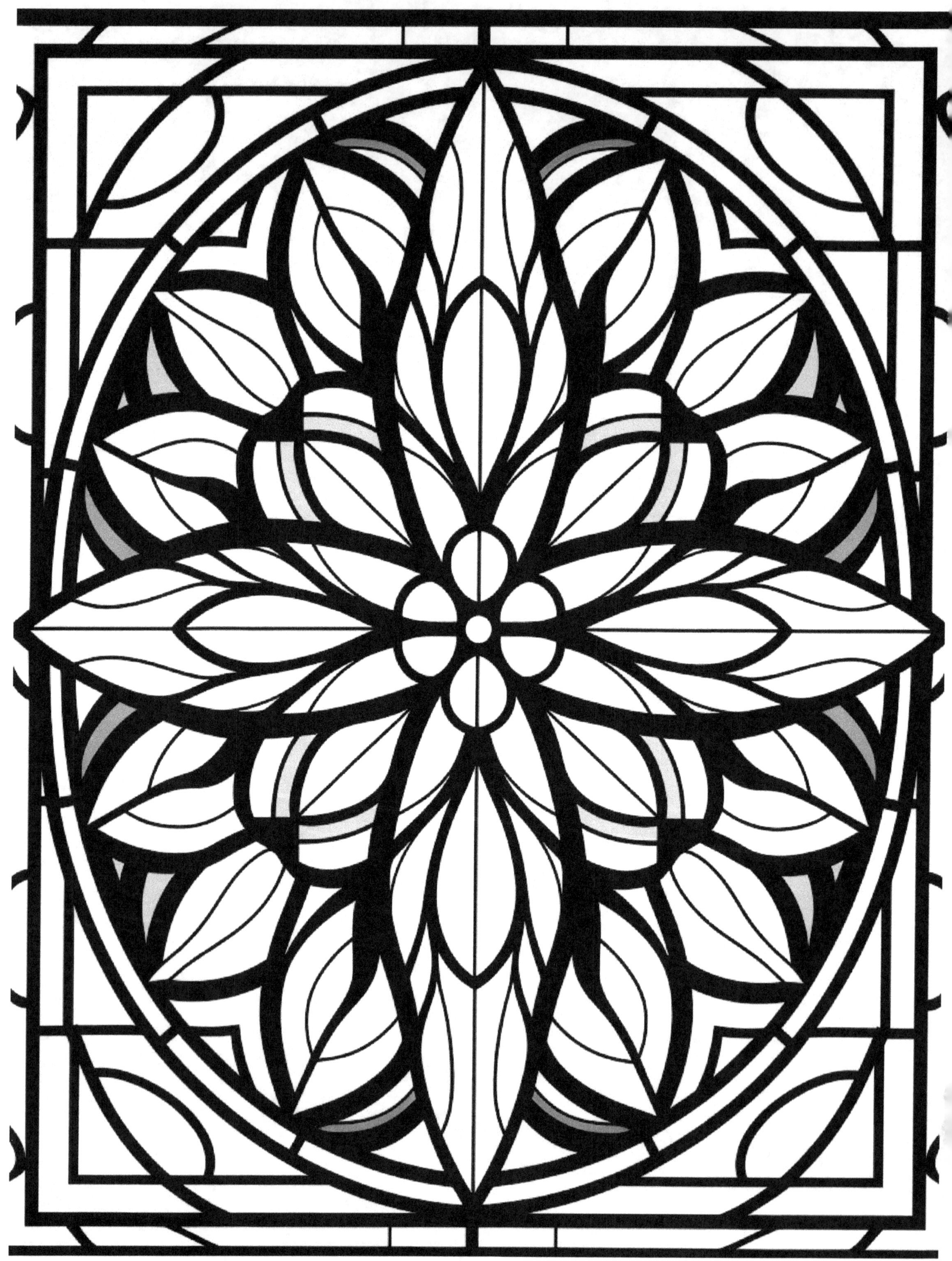

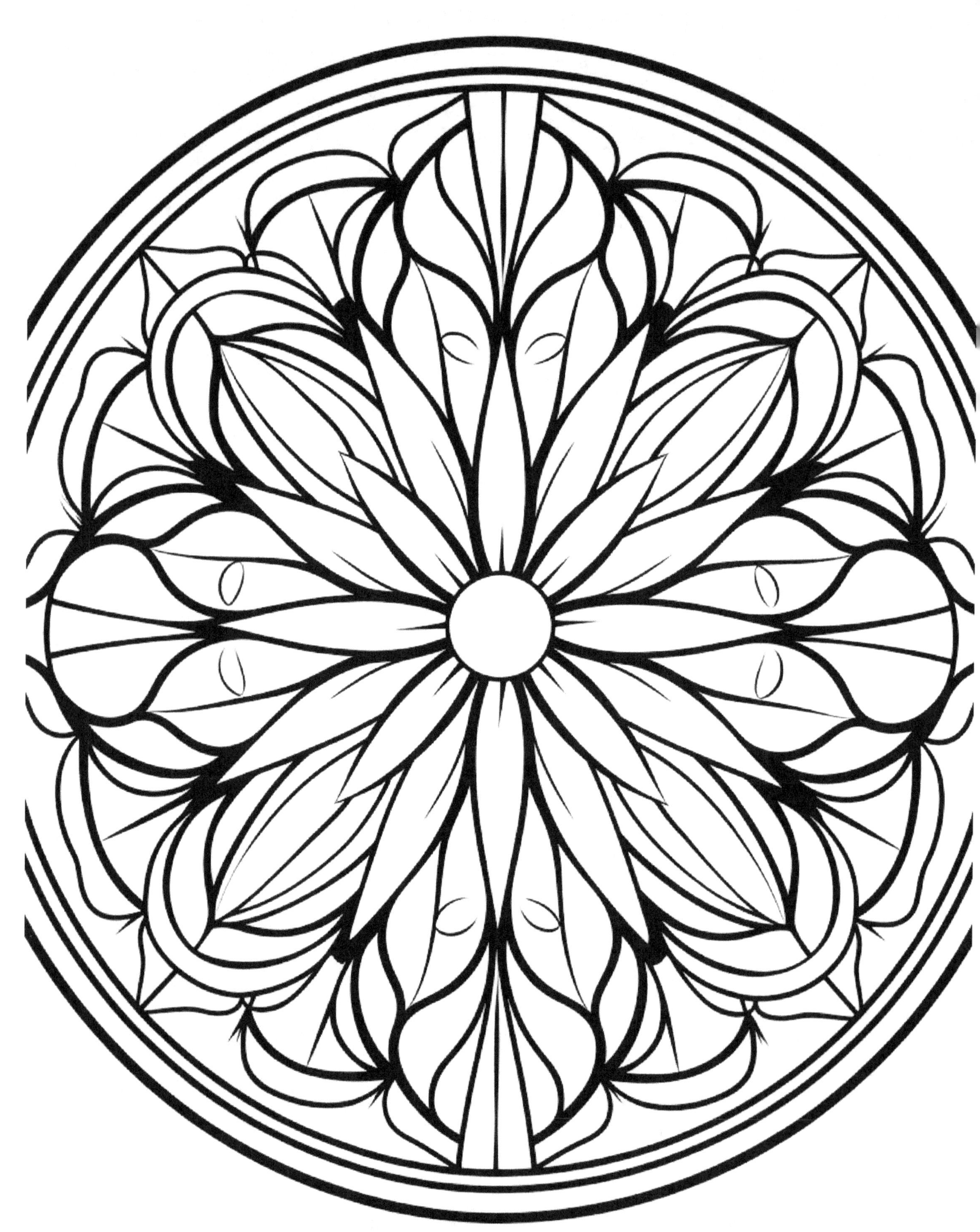

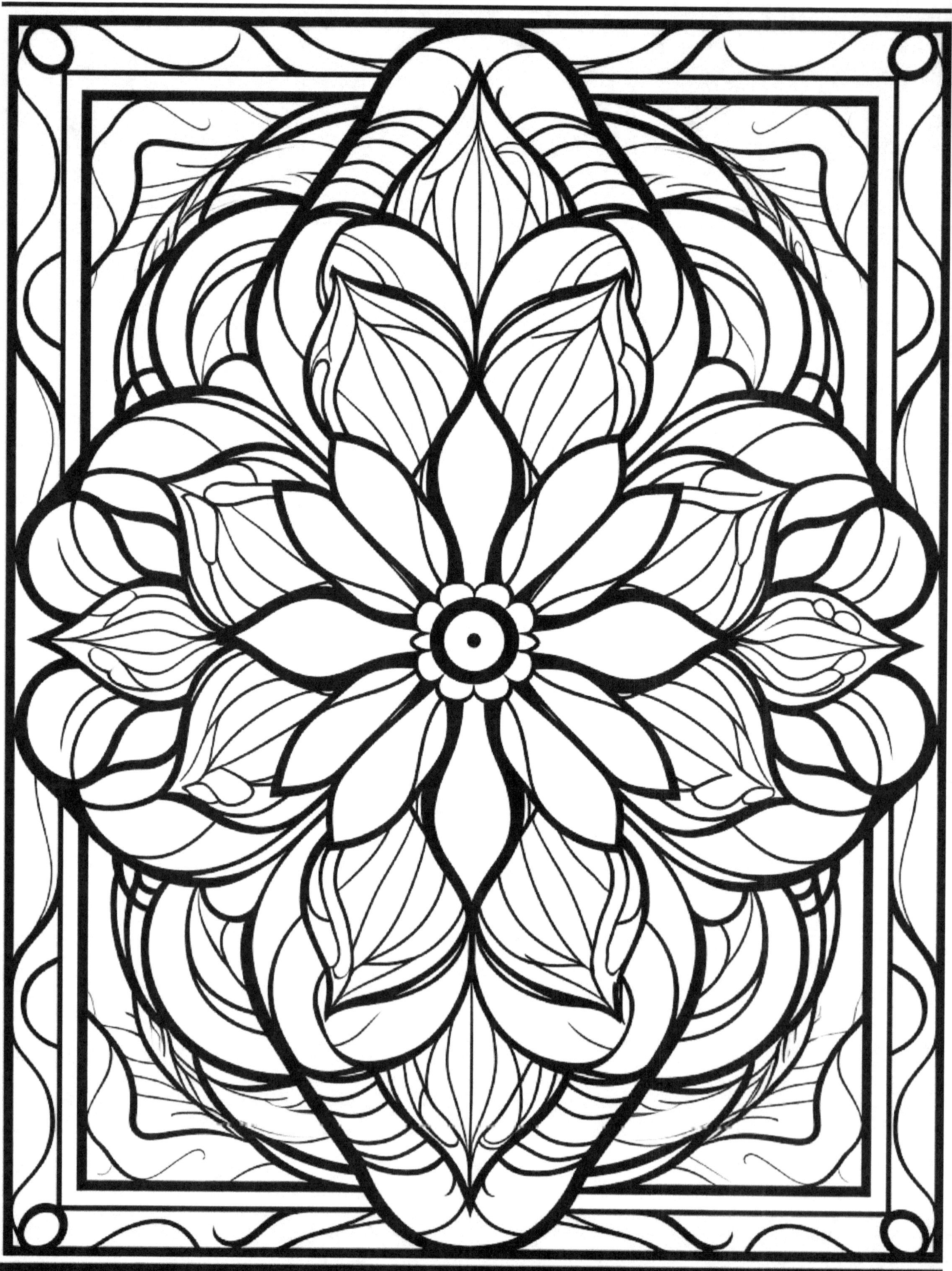

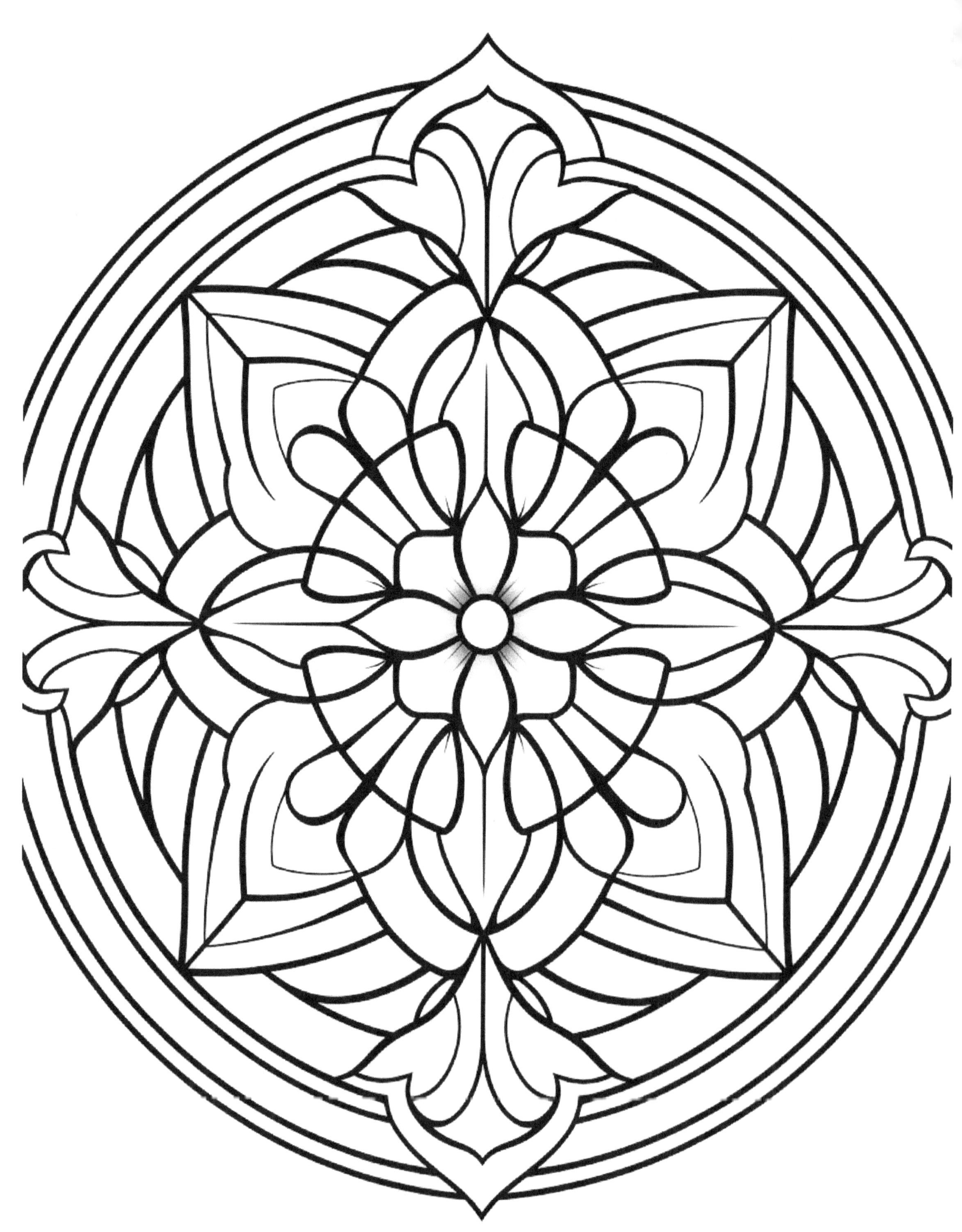

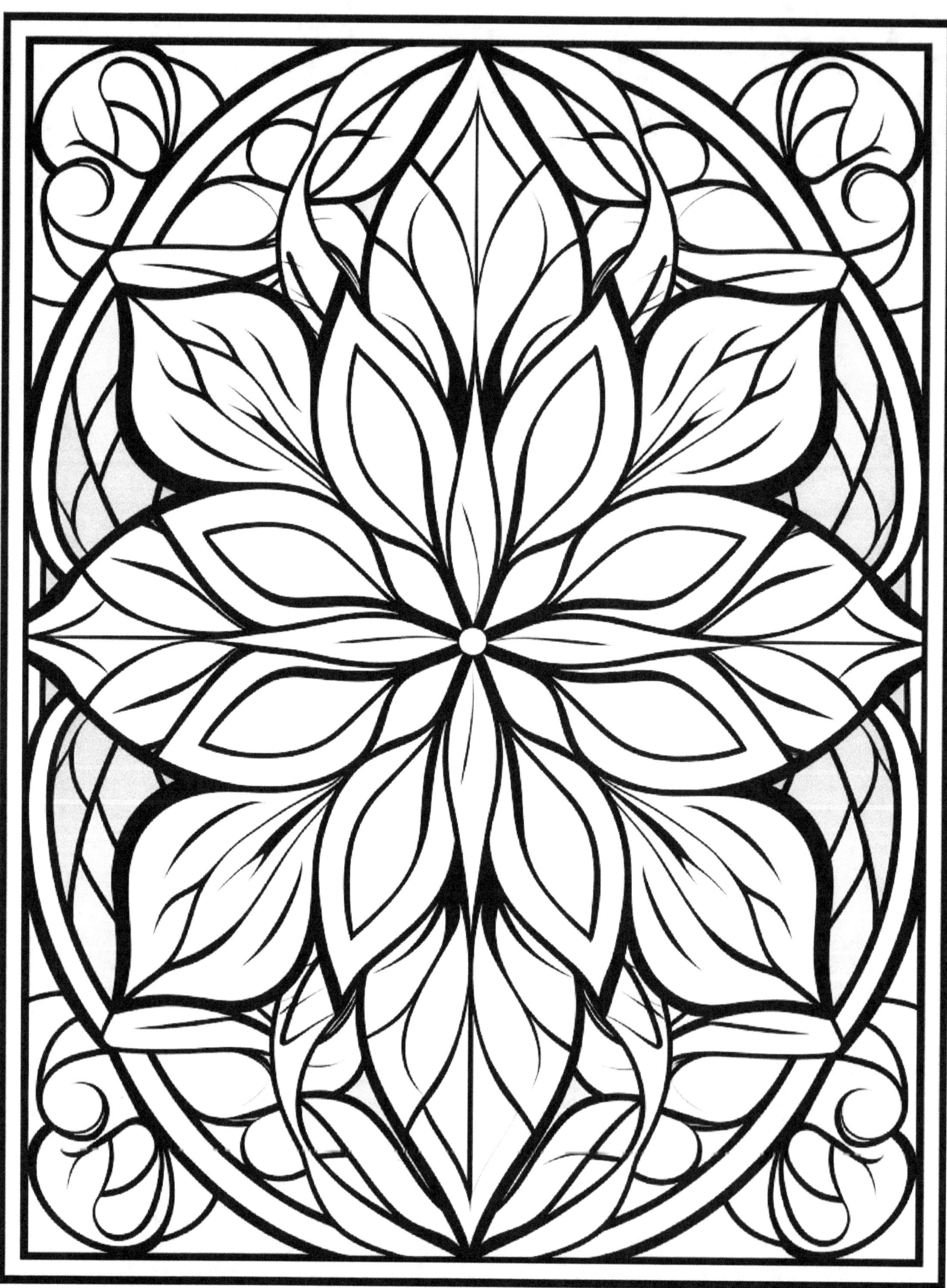

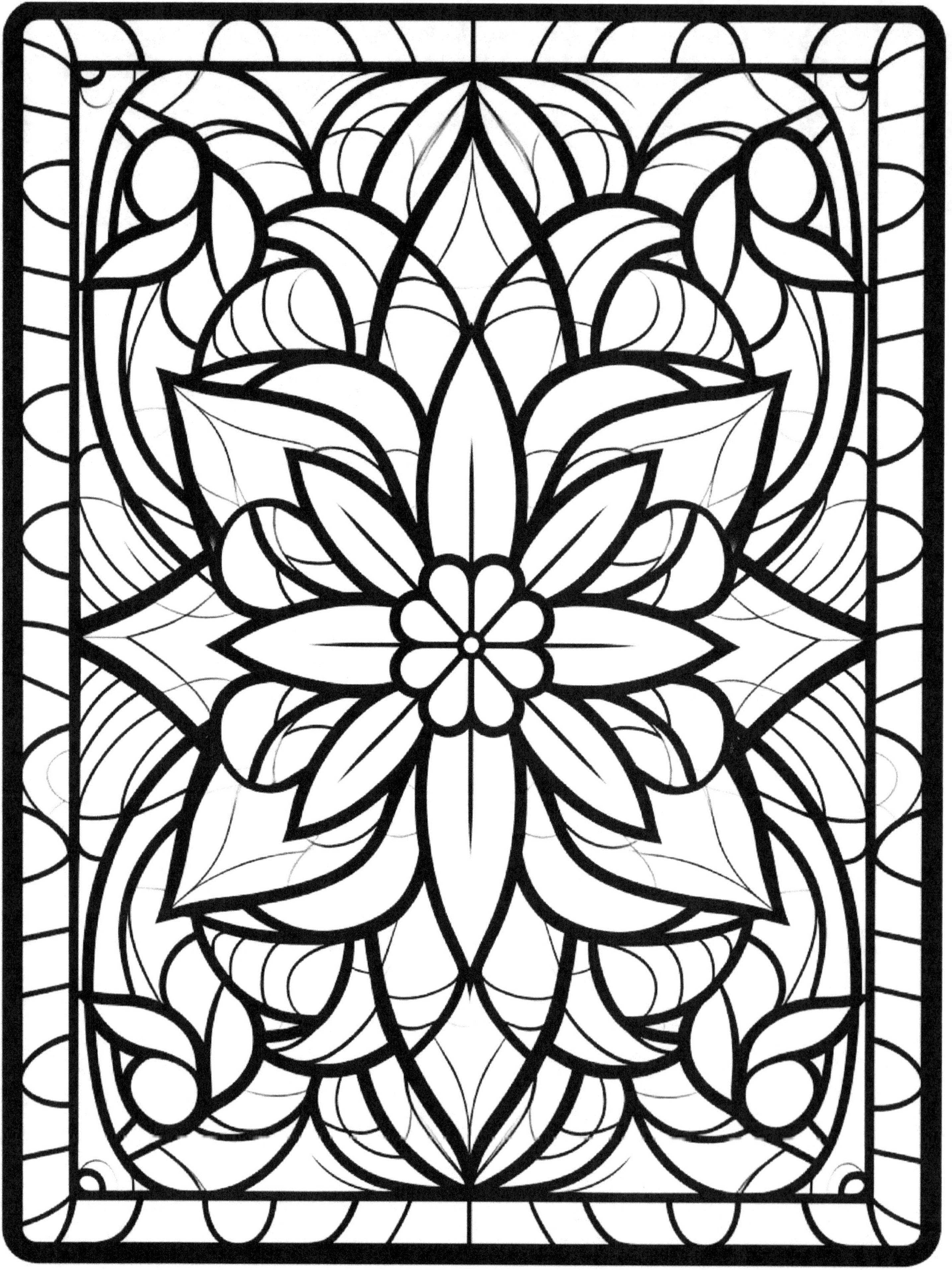

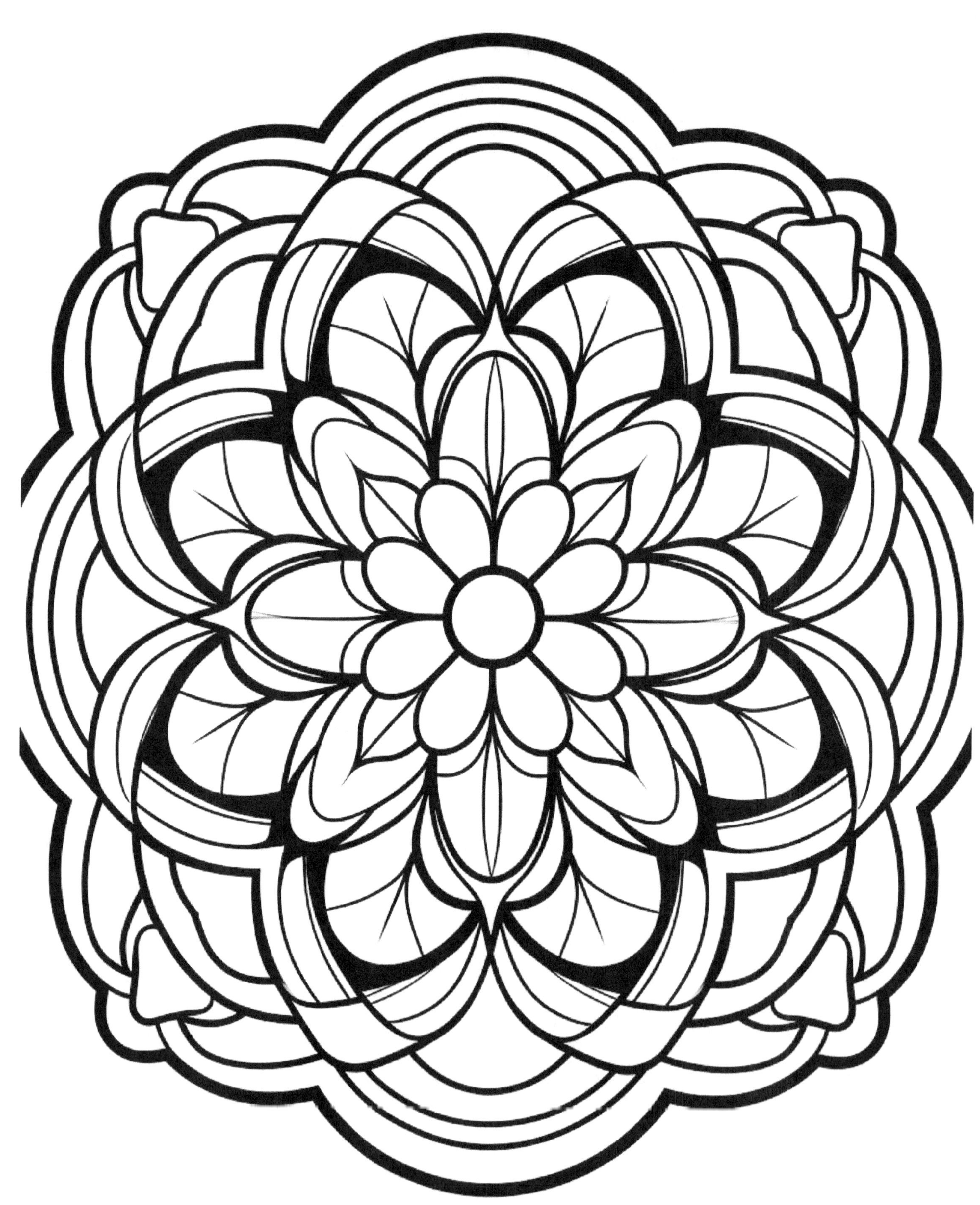

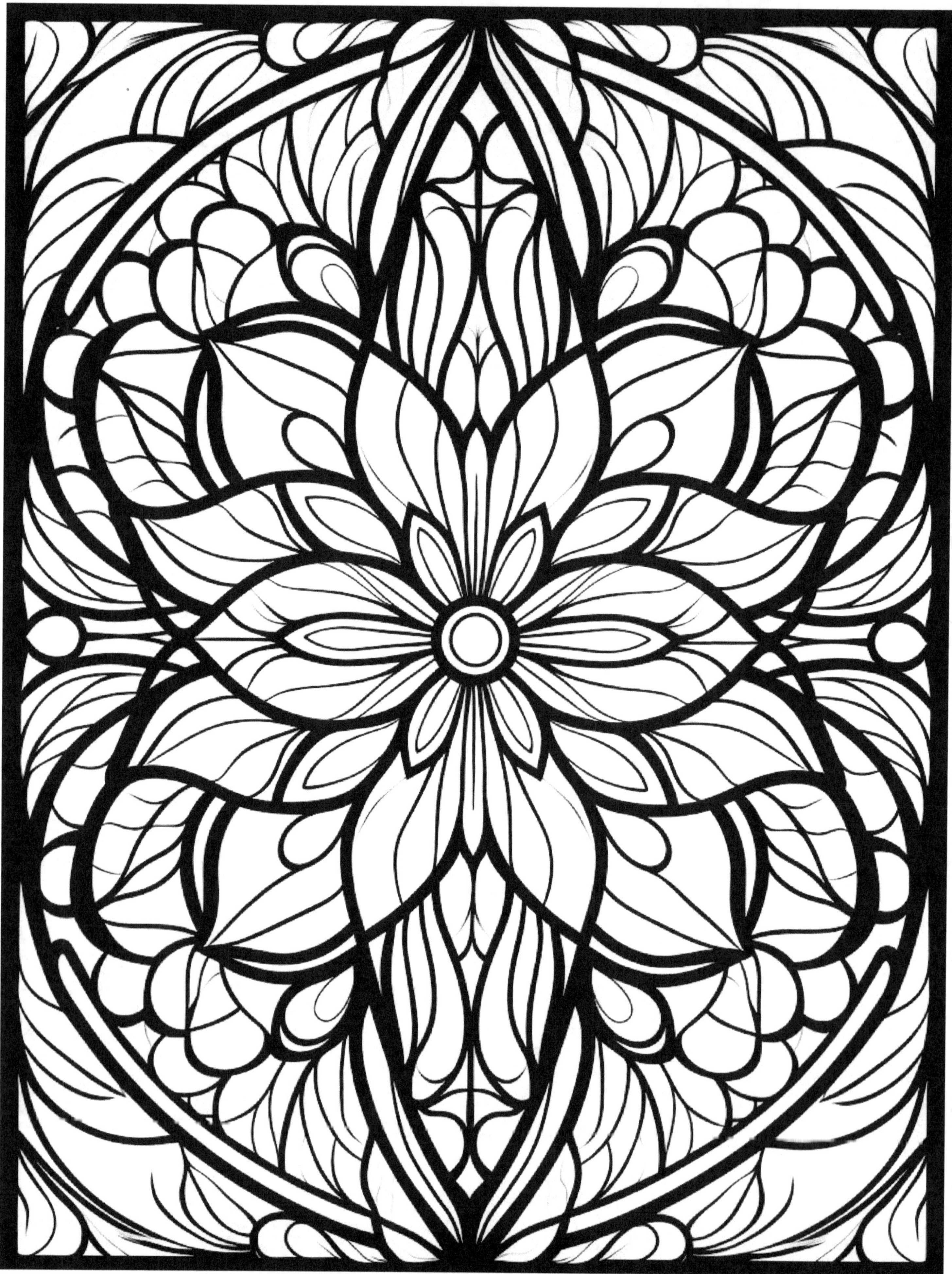

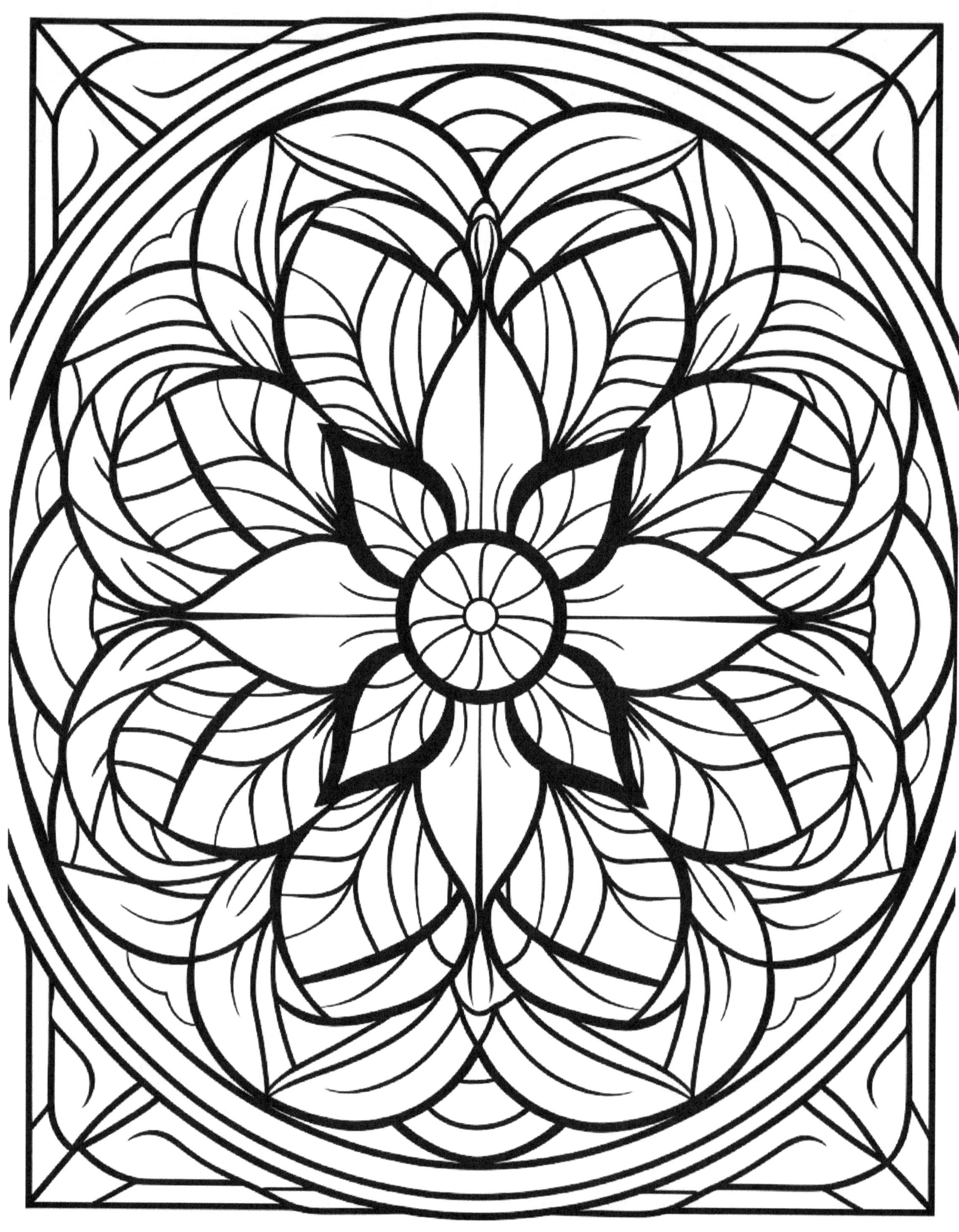

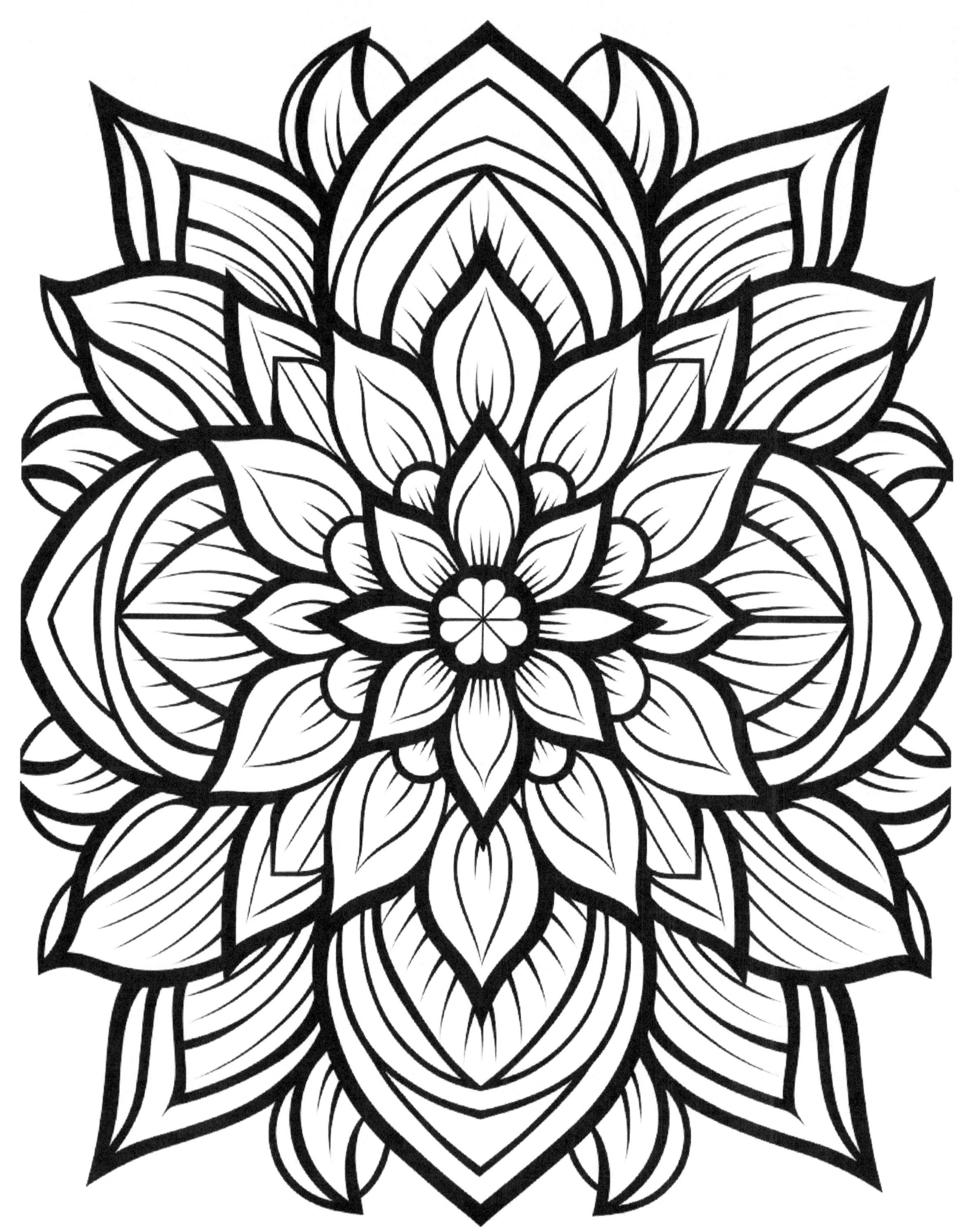

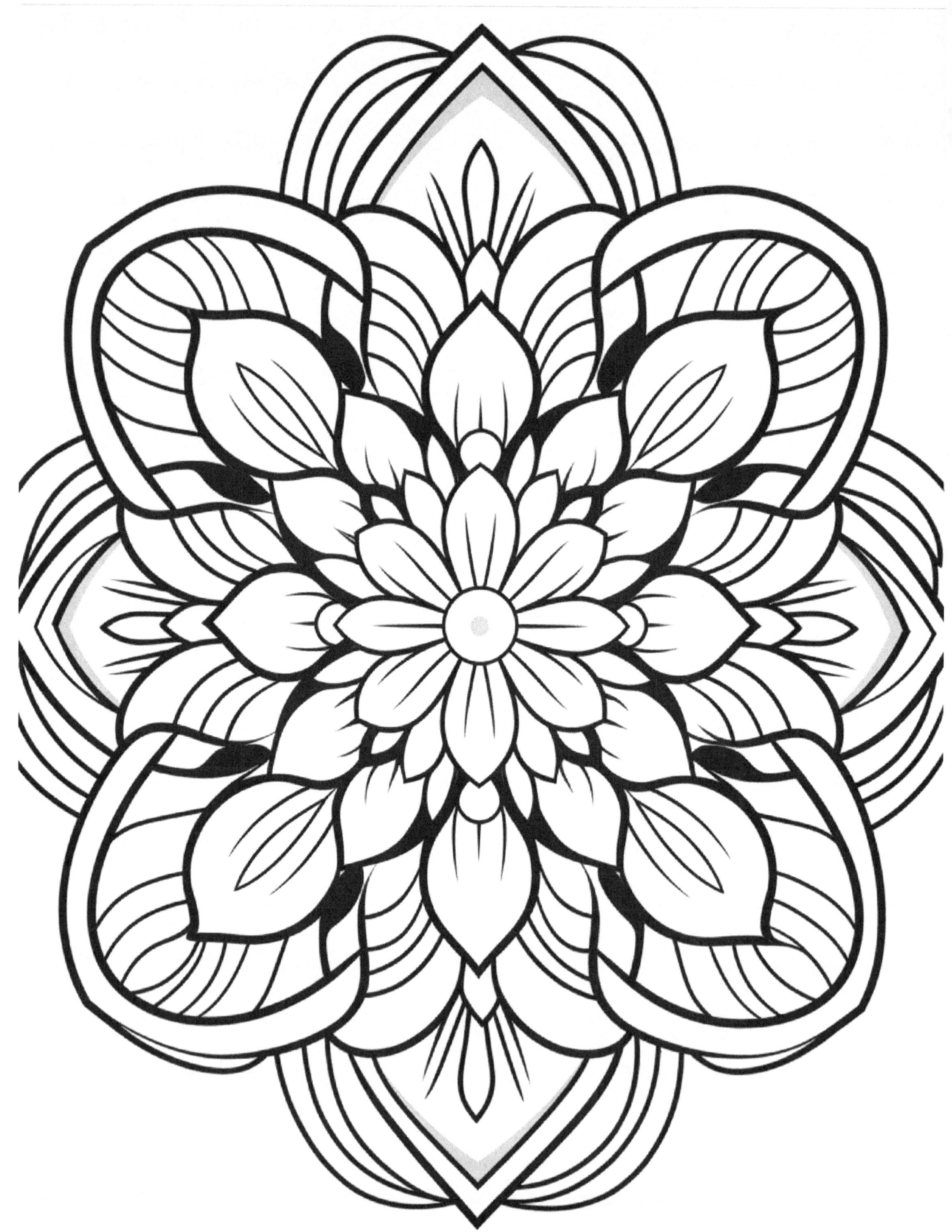